Praise for

"Reading this book has inspired me to be a better husband, father, grandfather, son, brother, neighbor, and covenant-keeping disciple of Jesus Christ! It has inspired me to remember the things that matter most."

—Jack R. Christianson, PhD, author, former director of the Orem Institute of Religion, and past executive administrator at Utah Valley University

"Alonzo Gaskill has produced a monumental work that every living soul should receive into their hearts. It will change your lives and provide direction and reminders to do as Jesus would do. . . . Remembering is the most important word in the English language for it ensures that we are about our Father's business. . . . Brother Gaskill has pointed out in his marvelous work a plethora of things that we need to remember. . . . I am sure all the prophets in the Book of Mormon would be pleased—especially King Benjamin, Mormon, and Moroni—as Brother Gaskill has helped all of us to remember."

—Ed J. Pinegar, former mission president, Provo MTC president, and past president of the Manti Temple

"It just may be that no word is of greater significance in scripture—and in life—than the word *remember*. Memory is an amazing, God-given gift, one that focuses us on what we once experienced, what we once felt, and what we once knew. When we remember—both blessings from obedience and painful consequences from disobedience—we are much less likely to wander from the path of goodness and decency. And when we strive to remember what our Savior has done for us, what an infinite price He paid, we are far more likely to live in a state of everlasting gratitude, which mindset empowers us to retain a remission of sins from day to day. In this important book, Alonzo Gaskill renders us a valuable service in emphasizing the kinds of things the Saints of the Most High simply must remember, if we are to qualify to go to that place where we see as we are seen and know as we are known."

—Robert L. Millet, professor emeritus of ancient scripture, Brigham Young University

Remember

∾ Sacred Truths We Must *Never* Forget ∾

ALONZO L. GASKILL

CFI
An Imprint of Cedar Fort, Inc.
Springville, Utah

ISBN 13: 978-1-4621-1465-8

Published by CFI, an imprint of Cedar Fort, Inc.
2373 W. 700 S., Springville, UT 84663
Distributed by Cedar Fort, Inc., www.cedarfort.com

LIBRARY OF CONGRESS CATALOGING-IN-PUBLICATION DATA

Gaskill, Alonzo L., author.
Remember : sacred things we must never forget / Alonzo L. Gaskill.
  pages cm
Includes bibliographical references.
ISBN 978-1-4621-1465-8 (alk. paper)
1. Christian life--Mormon authors. 2. Mormons--Conduct of life. 3. Conduct of life. 4. Church of Jesus Christ of Latter-day Saints--Doctrines. 5. Mormon Church--Doctrines. I. Title.

BX8656.G37 2015
248.4'89332--dc23

2015002696

Cover design by Shawnda T. Craig
Cover design © 2015 Lyle Mortimer
Edited and typeset by Jessica B. Ellingson

Printed in the United States of America

10 9 8 7 6 5 4 3 2 1

Printed on acid-free paper

To Rod Southwick, who inspired me
with the thought that became the book.

ᘁ Contents ᘁ

Acknowledgments ix

Introduction 1

REMEMBER: COVENANTS AND COMMANDMENTS

The Most Important Commandment 7

To Teach Principles and Let People
Govern Themselves 9

The Feelings of Guilt Associated with Sin 13

The Truth Is Painful for Those Who
Live Unrighteously 15

The Sabbath Day, to Keep It Holy 19

To Follow the Prophet 23

Your Temple Covenants 25

To Attend the Temple 27

That We Each Need a Savior 31

The Sacred Nature of the Sacrament 35

To Build Your Life upon Christ 39

REMEMBER: RELATIONSHIPS

Who You Are 45

Who Your Children Are 47

Your Family 51

The Counsel of Your Parents 53

To Love 55

To Forgive 57

To See Other People's Point of View 61

To Build Others 63

Don't Take Yourself or Life Too Seriously................... 67
What You Felt for Your Spouse
    When You Were Courting 71
Everything God Does Is for Your Good 73
What Truly Matters in Life 77
REMEMBER: CHURCH SERVICE
Not Everyone Is Where You Are Spiritually.................. 81
Your Duty 83
To Testify 87
The Name of Christ... 89
To Counsel 91
To Follow Promptings without Delay 93
It's Not about the Numbers 95
REMEMBER: LIVE A GODLY LIFE
To Pray..99
Gratitude in Prayer 103
The Captivity of Your Fathers 105
The Importance of Personal Scripture Study................ 109
Death 113
The Importance of Honesty.....................................115
Spiritual Experiences You've Had in the Past 119
Lot's Wife 123
To Be Patient with Yourself 127
Christ's Example of Ministering 129
That Your Temporal Gifts Do Not Belong to You 131
The Pioneers 135
How Blessed You Are.. 137
That Happiness Is a Choice 141
Notes 143
Bibliography.. 147
About the Author.. 150

∾ Acknowledgments ∾

I express my sincere appreciation to Drs. Robert L. Millet and Richard G. Moore for their thoughtful review of this manuscript and for their helpful suggestions. They are men of God whose lives exemplify the principles presented in this book.

∾ *Introduction* ᴄᴗ

*I*n one of his most famous apostolic talks, Elder Spencer W. Kimball suggested that the most important term in the dictionary might very well be the word *remember.*[1] The older I get, the more convinced I am of this gospel truth.

Covenants, commandments, and Christ have no effect in our lives if we fail to remember them. It is in remembering that we find the strength to resist evil and do what is right. It is in remembering the sacred things of God that they become holy to you and me. Hence, Moses warned ancient Israel, "Take heed unto yourselves, lest ye forget the covenant of the Lord your God, which he made with you" (Deuteronomy 4:23).

Every sin committed by us fallen mortals—both sins of commission *and* those of omission—can be directly attributed to the offender's failure to remember. When we choose to sin, we have either forgotten our covenants or we have failed to remember the consequences of breaking them. Thus time and again in disciplinary councils throughout the world, men and women tell the same sad story of sacred

promises forgotten and sins then committed. President Kimball noted:

> I guess we as humans are prone to forget. It is easy to forget. Our sorrows, our joys, our concerns, our great problems seem to wane to some extent as time goes on, and there are many lessons that we learn which have a tendency to slip from us. . . . I suppose there would never be an apostate, there would never be a crime, if people remembered, really remembered, the things they had covenanted at the water's edge or at the sacrament table and in the temple. I suppose that is the reason the Lord asked Adam to offer sacrifices, for no other reason than that he and his posterity would remember—remember the basic things that they had been taught.[2]

Church discipline and the potential loss of our salvation are not the only reasons we must remember. To forget our covenants or the commandments has a dramatic impact upon others. In forgetting, we fail to be faithful in our callings, or in our home and visiting teaching. In forgetting, we rear children who are not converted to the gospel of Jesus Christ. In forgetting, we let others down—family and friends. In forgetting, we fail to become like God and are thereby unable to bless His children as we might.

The strength of this Church is to be found in the commitment and faithfulness of its members. Through remembering, we become a celestial church. But as we collectively forget, the most we can hope for is a terrestrial reward. A church with members living at a terrestrial level can hardly save the world. Indeed, they cannot expect to be saved themselves.

This book is largely a collection of things we Latter-day Saints sometimes neglect, or altogether forget. Contained within the pages of this short work is an assortment of things that would bless our lives were we to faithfully remember them. While the list of topics presented is hardly exhaustive, were the readers to remember each of the principles taught herein, they would surely qualify for exaltation in the kingdom of God.

I invite you to join me in some brief introspection and self-evaluation. Together, as disciples of the Lord Jesus Christ, let's remember what God has asked of us and what we have covenanted to be. As you read, attend to the changes the Spirit encourages *you* to make. Pay particular attention to the principles that are *not* mentioned herein but that the Holy Ghost will encourage you individually to remember. The gift to remember—to notice, recall, and be grateful for—is a gift of the Spirit that God offers to any who seek it. President Henry B. Eyring recently indicated that "a gift of remembrance . . . comes though the gift of the Holy Ghost."[3] Similarly, the Lord has promised that the Spirit will "bring all things to your remembrance" (John 14:26). As you make a conscious choice to remember, you can be assured that the Lord will pour out His blessings and power upon you.

Remember

Covenants and Commandments

ᙣᎧ *Remember* ᥴᙩ

The Most Important Commandment

Over the years, I've heard various members of the Church refer to a variety of commandments as "the most important." For some, it is the law of chastity; for another, the law of tithing. An acquaintance of mine is emphatic that keeping the Sabbath day holy is the most important of the commandments. We all probably know someone in our ward who believes that doing family history is the most important of God's commands. You may have your own "favorite commandment" that you believe is the most important of all of God's laws.

President Harold B. Lee suggested, "The most important of all the commandments of God is that one that *you* are having the most difficulty keeping today."4 That being the case, it behooves each of us every day to remember what our personal weaknesses or challenges are and to work with

zeal to overcome them. Sins do not, of themselves, dissipate with time. They require effort, sacrifice, and focused attention. We must place our trust in God and in His power to transform us. To paraphrase the Lord: "If ye have faith as a grain of mustard seed, ye shall say unto this mountain [of addiction or to any sinful behavior], Remove hence to yonder place; and it shall remove; and nothing shall be impossible unto you. Howbeit this kind goeth not out but by prayer and fasting" (Matthew 17:20–21). We each have personal demons we battle or "pet sins" that remain for years at a time. A casual approach to repentance and change is never sufficient to enable us to overcome them. Because we love God, and because we have testimonies of His holy plan, we should daily remind ourselves of where our greatest weakness lies so that we can plot our coup against that sin or weakness. And because each of us ultimately hopes to dwell for eternity with God, having become like Him, we should fortify our lives from the source of our temptation and earnestly think about ways in which we can end the battle that rages within our soul.

∾ *Remember* ∾

To Teach Principles and Let People Govern Themselves

For some, *there* is something attractive about everything in the gospel being black and white. Grey areas require making decisions, and that brings accountability. There are always those who would rather not have to prayerfully consider options. Of course, the Lord has said, "For behold, it is not meet that I should command in all things; for he that is compelled in all things, the same is a slothful and not a wise servant; wherefore he receiveth no reward" (D&C 58:26).

On the other hand, there are also those within the Church who seek to be truer than true, who feel that the way *they* live a given commandment is the way *all* should live the commandments. For these folks, there might be things not specifically mentioned in the Word of Wisdom that they

think each of us should nevertheless avoid. They may have an opinion on tithes and offerings, or how to properly keep the Sabbath day holy. Perhaps they insist on vocalizing their higher standards, representing them as the Lord's standards, each time these pet subjects come up in church. We must be careful to avoid what President Joseph F. Smith referred to as "religious hobbies."[5]

The prophets and apostles have shown us how to approach commandments and the varied opinions regarding them. As a singular example, in defining what we should tithe, the First Presidency has explained that "members of the Church should pay 'one-tenth of all their interest annually,' which is understood to mean income. *No one is justified in making any other statement than this.*"[6] Instead of telling us whether we should pay tithing on the sweater Grandma gave us for Christmas, or on your gross versus net income, the Brethren have taught us a principle and then asked us to find the application in our own lives. As Spirit-directed Latter-day Saints, we should not need to be counseled in all things, nor should we feel a need to impose our views on others. How you pay tithing or live the Word of Wisdom (or keep any other commandment) is between you and the Lord. When we seek to obtain a temple recommend, we will be asked, "Are you a full-tithe payer?" But the interviewer will not ask, "Do you pay tithing on gifts you receive?" The principles and laws of the gospel should be lived, but in large measure the Lord leaves it to us to prayerfully ascertain how we might best do so. That being the case, we should follow His example by remembering that what the Spirit reveals to us may not be *exactly* what it reveals to someone else. This by no means suggests that the commandments and standards of the Church are relative. But each of us has different circumstances and different needs. The Lord knows that, and He reveals and inspires accordingly.

Like those who preside over the work today, the Prophet Joseph indicated that his approach to governing the Saints was as follows: "I teach the people correct principles and they govern themselves."[7] As leaders, parents, or simply members of a ward or quorum, when we teach, we should teach principles and let our hearers—under the influence of the Spirit—govern themselves in the application. Remembering this approach not only reduces disagreements and contention, it also ensures that members become moral agents who have the opportunity to discover for themselves how the Lord would have them live His laws.

❧ Remember ❧

The Feelings of Guilt
Associated with Sin

Many years ago, I was playing the drums in a marching band during a bitterly cold January Cotton Bowl event. Because of the frigid weather, I was unable to feel my hands. As I was playing, unbeknownst to me, I hit my knuckle several times on the metal rims of the drums. Initially, I felt no pain and my hands didn't bleed because the cold had numbed me. After the performance, however, when my hands began to warm, my knuckles began to bleed and the pain in my hands became quite significant.

Our nerve endings are a gift from God. They allow us to feel, but they also protect us from harming ourselves by sending messages to our brain in the form of pain. Were this not the case, each of us would severely injure ourselves

in a variety of ways. Like nerve endings, guilt is also a gift from God. The palpable feelings associated with the loss of the Spirit or with the need to repent help us desire to remain aloof from sin. The Prophet Joseph rightly taught, "Those who have done wrong always have that wrong gnawing them. . . . You cannot go anywhere but where God can find you out."[8] Alma the Younger bore witness to this truth when he declared, "I did remember all my sins and iniquities, for which I was tormented with the pains of hell" (Alma 36:13).

Unfortunately, some sinners are like the "fool" described in the proverb, "As a dog returneth to his vomit, so a fool returneth to his folly" (Proverbs 26:11). While we must let go of the sins of the past for which we have sincerely repented, we must never forget the darkness and pain associated with the loss of the Spirit and the cost and consequences of sin. In addition, we must also remember how difficult true repentance is; we cannot step away from the path and expect to find that all has stood still while we were gone. Remembering the pain that our past sinful choices have caused us will limit our willingness to embrace the enticings of the adversary in the future.

⨯ Remember ⨯

The Truth Is Painful for Those
Who Live Unrighteously

Laman and Lemuel are the poster children for those who murmur. I can almost hear their pathetic, whining voices declare to their father, "It is a hard thing which you require of us!" (see 1 Nephi 3:5). Murmuring is evidence of the weakness of one's position. We murmur because we know "not the dealings of that God who had created [us]" (1 Nephi 2:12). We also murmur because we dare not boldly articulate our views, for we know in our hearts we are wrong. Nephi describes the condition of the hearts of his brothers—a condition we have all encountered in the lives of others, and perhaps also in our own:

> And now it came to pass that after I, Nephi, had made an end of speaking to my brethren, behold they said unto me:

Thou hast declared unto us hard things, more than we are able to bear.

And it came to pass that I said unto them that I knew that I had spoken hard things against the wicked, according to the truth; and the righteous have I justified, and testified that they should be lifted up at the last day; wherefore, *the guilty taketh the truth to be hard, for it cutteth them to the very center.*

And now my brethren, if ye were righteous and were willing to hearken to the truth, and give heed unto it, that ye might walk uprightly before God, then ye would not murmur because of the truth, and say: Thou speakest hard things against us. (1 Nephi 16:1–3; emphasis added)

Jacob similarly testified: "O, my beloved brethren, give ear to my words. Remember the greatness of the Holy One of Israel. Do not say that I have spoken hard things against you; for if ye do, ye will revile against the truth; for I have spoken the words of your Maker. *I know that the words of truth are hard against all uncleanness*; but the righteous fear them not, for they love the truth and are not shaken" (2 Nephi 9:40; emphasis added). No truer words were ever spoken than these from the lips of Nephi and Jacob.

What a gift from God that feelings of hurt come to us when our position is not the Lord's position. When the truth is proclaimed, if we are found on the opposite side from the Lord, God grants us a forceful opportunity to reconsider, repent, and conform. If the words of the Presiding Brethren rub us wrong, we would do well to remember the teachings of Nephi and Jacob. If the advice of the Apostles "cuts us to the very center" or feels "hard" to our hearts, this is the

Spirit testifying to our spirits that we are in need of repentance. What a glorious gift, enabling us to always know if our wills are aligned with God's. Will we respond as would Nephi and Jacob? Or will we respond, with Laman and Lemuel, "It is a hard thing which you require of us"?

❦ Remember ❧

The Sabbath Day, to Keep It Holy

Upon *Mount Sinai,* from the finger of Jehovah, Moses received the Decalogue—better known as the Ten Commandments. Among other things given for their spiritual safety and well-being, covenant Israel was commanded to "remember the sabbath day, to keep it holy" (Exodus 20:8; Mosiah 13:16). Indeed, as with all of the commandments of God, the mandate that the covenant people honor the Sabbath was offered as a blessing, a gift to God's people from their loving Father. It was given as a shield and protection against temptation and sin.

The word *Sabbath* comes from the Hebrew verb "to rest." The implication is that on this day, we rest from our labors. We do not rest from labors of love and service but from worldly labors and the concern for secular things. As the old colloquialism goes, "The way to sanctify a day is to

let the day sanctify us." Thus, the Sabbath is largely about our need for rest from worldliness and sin. It is about forgetting "me" and thinking about "Him" (God) and "them" (His children whom we can and should serve). St. Augustine frequently taught that the Sabbath "imposes a regular periodical holiday—quietness of heart, tranquility of mind, the product of a good conscience. Here is sanctification, because here is the Spirit of God."[9] In other words, because the Sabbath provokes the presence of the Spirit, it sanctifies us from sin, and it changes our fallen natures. As we remember the Sabbath and keep it holy, the consequence is that our lives become more holy and temptations lose much of their power over us. The converse is also true: if we fail to keep the Sabbath as a holy day, the world will have a greater and greater presence in our lives, and temptations will become more and more enticing to us.

In what seems a rather shocking dictate, the Lord declared, "Ye shall keep the sabbath; . . . for it is holy unto you: every one that defileth it shall surely be put to death: for whosoever doeth any work therein, that soul shall be cut off from among his people. Six days may work be done; but in the seventh is the sabbath of rest, holy to the Lord: whosoever doeth any work in the sabbath day, he shall surely be put to death" (Exodus 31:14–15). Today we do not put Sabbath-breakers to death, but we do acknowledge that those who do not seek to observe a weekly Sabbath put themselves to death spiritually. They cut themselves off from the Lord's Spirit and often from the Lord's Church. Thus, like a parent who warns a child about dangers, the Father has warned us about the risks of not having a day of devotion wherein we can recharge our spiritual batteries and through which we can purge ourselves of the influences of the world.

The Sabbath was designed by the Lord to be a joy, but we run the risk of turning it into a burden if we become Pharisaical about how we live it and what we expect of others on it. The Lord, through the prophet Isaiah, indicated that when we keep the Sabbath holy, we will earnestly be able to "call the sabbath a delight" (Isaiah 58:13). However, if our focus is mostly on rules and regulations, or the letter of the law, the Sabbath will become a burden rather than a blessing. As the Apostle Paul reminded us, "The letter killeth, but the spirit giveth life" (2 Corinthians 3:6).

We would benefit by remembering that the difference between a *holiday* and a *holy day* is the *i*. If we make the Sabbath about honoring God and serving His children—rather than about doing *our* own ways, finding *our* own pleasure, and speaking *our* own words (see Isaiah 58:13)—God will endow us with the strength to overcome all things.

✑ Remember ✐

To Follow the Prophet

O ver *the years*, the occasional student has asked me, "How do we know when the prophet is speaking the words of the Lord and when he is simply speaking his own opinion?" My response is typically something akin to this: "In light of the fact that these Brethren have been faithfully living the gospel for eight or nine decades, I don't think you need to worry yourself about that. Even if something they share is personal opinion, I think their opinions are pretty safe—well tried and tested." I'm *not* suggesting we exercise blind faith, but I *am* suggesting there is a reason why God has placed the man He has as President of the Church. Each of the men currently serving in the First Presidency and Quorum of the Twelve Apostles are there for a reason. Certainly part of that is because the Lord trusts their judgment. He knows they will lead and counsel

in accordance with the dictates of the Spirit. Thus, we can trust them. As President Wilford Woodruff reminded the Saints, "The Lord will never permit me or any other man who stands as President of this Church to lead you astray. It is not in the programme. It is not in the mind of God. If I were to attempt that, the Lord would remove me out of my place, and so He will any other man who attempts to lead the children of men astray from the oracles of God and from their duty" (Official Declaration 1). We can *always* trust the counsel of the prophet.

The author of the book of Hebrews offered this sound counsel concerning the example and advice of the prophets, seers, and revelators that God has placed to govern His work: "Remember your leaders, who spoke the word of God to you. Consider the outcome of their way of life and imitate their faith" (Hebrews 13:7, New International Version). In other words, follow their teachings, remember where the way they lived their lives has led them, and emulate their example. In so doing, you will be richly blessed. As the chorus to the children's song "Follow the Prophet" enjoins us:

> Follow the prophet, follow the prophet,
> Follow the prophet; don't go astray.
> Follow the prophet, follow the prophet,
> *Follow the prophet; he knows the way.*[10]

We often do not see what they see. We may not know what they know. But *if* we can muster the faith to trust in their words, remember their counsel, and follow their examples, the Lord promises to guide and protect us.

✤ Remember ✤

Your Temple Covenants

Years ago while watching the news, I learned of the excommunication of a rather well-known Latter-day Saint. He was not a general authority, but his excommunication made national news because of his prominence.

Tragically, this brother had an affair, which resulted in great suffering and significant losses for many people. When I heard the report on the news, the first thing that went through my mind was, "What about his temple garments?" I was puzzled how a man who had made sacred covenants in the house of the Lord—and who carried a token or reminder of those covenants upon his person at all times—could forget those covenants during a moment of temptation. After all, isn't that the point of the garments: to remind us of what we have promised God, so that we would not sin?

Years later, I was home teaching a brother, and somehow during the visit the subject of temple garments came up. The brother said to me, "Alonzo, they're just underwear!" I responded, "If that's all you think they are, then they have no power to protect you."

Covenants and symbols only have power if we endow them with meaning. If we make promises to God in the temple but then never contemplate the meaning or implication of those promises, they will have power to damn us, but not to save us. If we do not contemplate the symbolism of the clothing or the manner in which covenants are conveyed and made, then we miss the point of what the Lord is trying to teach us—what He is trying to share with us. Once again, these covenants will be powerless as they relate to helping us overcome the world.

For the temple and its ordinances and covenants to have power in our personal lives, we must remember them. And in order to remember them, we need to contemplate them. Blessings come to those who seek to understand their symbolic nature. We should endeavor to find meaning that resonates with us, and then that meaning will come to us in our hour of temptation or need.

∽ Remember ∾

To Attend the Temple

Each *Sunday when* I give temple recommend interviews, after the interview is over I will typically ask, "Are you able to get to the temple very often?" About 99 percent of the time, the response is, "Not as often as I should." Many Latter-day Saints are endowed but do not possess a current temple recommend. Even more carry a recommend but do not use it regularly. The temple and its covenants have no power in our lives, nor power to move us toward exaltation, if we do not regularly attend after receiving the endowment or being sealed to our spouse.

The most common excuses for not attending the temple include, "We're just so busy," and, "The month just flies by. We intended to go, but it just didn't happen." I often hear couples say, "We can't afford a babysitter," or, "Our schedules are so opposite of each other, we barely have time together,

ALONZO L. GASKILL

let alone time to go to the temple." Of course, there are ways around each of these roadblocks.

Busyness is about priorities and scheduling. We can always make time for something important to us. If we care about our covenants, we make time to live them by attending the temple regularly and consistently.

The month gets away from us when we don't have a set day and time to attend the temple. However, if the 7:00 p.m. session on the third Thursday of the month is *your* session, then the month won't "just get away from you," because that will be part of your standard schedule.

As a young couple, my wife and I did not typically have money for a sitter. Throughout the Church, many couples with young children participate in babysitting co-ops, where they trade babysitting for a night at the temple. Many of the youth in your ward will also babysit for free, or for a reduced cost, so that you can attend the temple.

The fact that a husband and wife have opposite schedules should not be a hindrance to attending the temple. If your spouse can't go with you this month, go on your own. After all, you don't sit together anyway! Getting to the temple regularly is even more important than doing so with one's spouse. Being there together is the ideal. But not going because one's spouse can't go is unwise.

Each of us needs in our personal lives the influence of the Spirit, which comes from attending the temple. We live in a world that barrages us with messages that are patently false. The house of the Lord has a spirit about it that endows us with power to see things as they really are. If we remember to go regularly, the adversary's influence in our lives will be greatly reduced, and the blessings conditionally pronounced upon us in the ordinances of the temple will become a reality. If we forget or neglect to attend, however, those rich offerings may never be realized.

❧ *Remember* ❧

That We Each Need a Savior

At the onset of the Sermon on the Mount, the Lord commanded His disciples, "Be ye therefore perfect, even as your Father which is in heaven is perfect" (Matthew 5:48). This divine dictate has overwhelmed many whose quest for perfection has left them discouraged as they daily strive for the personally unobtainable.

Of course, by "perfect" Jesus did not mean "flawless" or "sinless." We all know that there has only been one perfect man, and He never commands us to do impossible things (see 1 Nephi 3:7). Owing to the fact that no one other than Jesus has ever obtained complete moral perfection during his or her earthly sojourn, this is clearly not an obtainable mortal goal. So what does Jesus ask of us? The Greek word translated as "perfect" is more accurately rendered as "whole," "upright," "true," "faithful," "single-minded," "finished," or

"complete." But it does not suggest perfection, and certainly not perfectionism. Indeed, shortly after this call to better ourselves, Jesus noted that the "blessed" ones *still* "hunger and thirst after righteousness" (Matthew 5:6). What God is asking of us is not mortal perfection but a desire to be perfected by Him. He seeks in us a demeanor that is "true" or "faithful" to what we know to be right, one that motivates us to act like God because it fills us with grace and mercy toward others. Significantly, the Greek word *teleos* (translated as "perfect" in Matthew 5) has a future referent, so the scripture reads more like this: "Because of the things mentioned in the Sermon on the Mount, you will become perfect like your Father in Heaven." Thus, Jesus's words may have been intended as less of a command and more of a promise that through obedience to God's commands, He will make us perfect.

In view of this discussion of perfection, what's most worrisome is the common tendency for Latter-day Saints to acknowledge that they are saved by grace but then to conclude that they are exalted by their works. Which of us honestly believes that we can do sufficient good works to merit a place in the celestial kingdom of our God? Does anyone who truly grasps the sinful and fallen nature of man really believe that he or she has the ability to "earn" a place in God's presence? Hugh Nibley famously declared, "Work we must, but the lunch is free!"[11] In other words, while works of righteousness are a testament of our love for God and our belief in His plan, they do not have the power to save—largely because even the very best of us can never do enough to quality for a place in heaven. As the hymn "Come, Come, Ye Saints" asks, "Why should we think to earn a great reward?" (*Hymns*, no. 30). While we must not "shun the fight," we must also remember that we each desperately need a Savior—a Redeemer willing to purchase or buy us back from the enemy, who seeks to "seal [us] his" (Alma 34:35).

The line between carrying one's weight and spiritual self-sufficiency is thin. The Lord would certainly have us take responsibility for our choices and our personal spirituality. He would have us never forget, however, that *after all we can do*—meaning, above and beyond all we can do—it will yet be by *grace* that we are saved (see 2 Nephi 25:23). If we rely upon our own merits for salvation, we are hopelessly doomed. If, on the other hand, we remember Him and the promises He has made to all those who seek Him, then through His grace and mercy we shall one day find ourselves exalted in the kingdom of God. Praise be God for His goodness and unfailing love! And shame on us if we forget that we cannot, and should not, try to do this alone.

∽ Remember ∾

The Sacred Nature of the Sacrament

The most sacred event of the week for practicing Latter-day Saints is sacrament meeting. And the most important part of that meeting—the portion that should be our focus—is not the sermons but rather the administration of the sacrament. We should prepare ourselves spiritually and mentally before we partake. And as we partake of the blessed bread and water, we should do so with a spirit of reverence and contemplation.

A quarter of a century ago, I read a book that chronicled the events of Christ's Atonement, particularly what He suffered on behalf of each of us in Gethsemane's Garden and upon Golgotha's cross. After writing about these sacred events with some detail and, at times, somewhat graphically, the authors made this point: "And we, two millennia later, spend 2.3 minutes per week considering this."[12] I remember

being a bit taken back by this. Admittedly, most of us do not spend the time in preparation, contemplation, and anticipation that we should—owing to the fact that partaking of the sacrament actually has the power to apply the atoning blood of Christ in our lives and thereby forgive our sins. At the moment we sincerely and humbly partake, the sins of the past week are purged from our souls and from the records of heaven, and we become clean, just as we were the day we were baptized. If anything qualifies as a miracle, this does. And yet, for some of us, that thought never crosses our minds when we partake. For many, various distractions hold their attention more than this sacred reality does. The concern seems more about which piece of bread they'll chose than which sin they are most sorrowful for, most committed to overcoming. Truly, 2.3 minutes simply isn't enough!

As He introduced His first-century disciples to the sacrament of the Lord's Supper, Jesus said to them, "This do in remembrance of me" (Luke 22:19). This strikes me as a commandment. Our Lord did not say, "If you would like, feel free to remember me as you partake." He wants His disciples to contemplate what those emblems mean, both symbolically and individually as they seek forgiveness for the sins and failings of the past. When introducing this same ordinance to the Nephites, Jesus added this promise: "And if ye do always remember me ye shall have my Spirit to be with you" (3 Nephi 18:7). Our Lord promises us His Spirit, and His Spirit sanctifies. It cleanses us. It makes us holy.

Christ would have us remember that our salvation came at great cost. We were bought with a price that is

incomprehensible to you and me. And while we cannot fathom what He went through for us, individually or collectively, we *can* grasp that His sacrifice, symbolized by the sacrament, was the ultimate act of love for individuals unworthy of that gift. And with that sobering thought, we can resolve to be better this week than we were the week before; not for the sake of a promised reward, but because we love Him for loving us first (1 John 4:19).

∾ ℛemember ∾

To Build Your Life upon Christ

---

*I*n a *discourse* where he employs the word *remember* some fifteen times, Helaman—the father of Nephi and Lehi—counseled his sons:

> And now, my sons, remember, remember that it is upon the rock of our Redeemer, who is Christ, the Son of God, that ye must build your foundation; that when the devil shall send forth his mighty winds, yea, his shafts in the whirlwind, yea, when all his hail and his mighty storm shall beat upon you, it shall have no power over you to drag you down to the gulf of misery and endless wo, because of the rock upon which ye are built, which is a sure foundation, a foundation whereon if men build they cannot fall. (Helaman 5:12; see also Psalm 78:35).

Helaman indicates that when we build our lives upon Christ, those inevitable storms that come to us all lose their

power and their influence. A life built upon Christ is powerful, strong, enduring, and faith-filled. We are certainly aware of the storms of mortality, but we are not harmed by them.

The phrase "building your life upon Christ" carries several connotations. It suggests that we seek to build or develop in ourselves the attributes of Christ. It implies that we seek to do the works of Jesus. Building upon Christ means we focus on Him above and beyond the many other pressing concerns of life. It means that we develop the "mind of Christ" (1 Corinthians 2:16). And once we have the "mind of Christ," we begin to "think what He thinks, know what He knows, say what He would say, and do what He would do in every situation—all by revelation from the Spirit."[13]

In the temple, when a couple enters into the new and everlasting covenant of marriage and is sealed for time and all eternity, they kneel at an altar across from each other. Altars are ancient symbols for Christ and His sacrifice. The placement of that primordial emblem between the two being sealed is a profound symbolic statement as to how to make the marriage work. The reality is implied that if they build their marriage upon Christ, it will succeed. Just as the altar is between them during the sealing ceremony, so also Christ must be kept central to the marriage for it to flourish. If the marriage is built upon Christ, and if both partners are willing to sacrifice for each other—keeping Him central to their personal lives—then that marriage will have the power to endure the storms of life. Such is the case with any aspect of our lives. If Christ is central, blessings abound.

The ordinances of the house of the Lord are saturated with symbols of Christ. Why? Because our Heavenly Father wishes to remind us at every turn of the importance of building our lives upon Christ. The temple teaches us how to cast Lucifer out of our lives, and it does so by teaching us how to build our lives upon our Redeemer. As we "always remember Him" (Moroni 5:2), the devil will have "no power . . . to drag [us] down to the gulf of misery and endless wo" (Helaman 5:12).

∽ Relationships ∾

✧ Remember ✧

Who You Are

It *has become* somewhat of a colloquialism within the Church for parents to say to their sons or daughters heading out for an evening with friends, "Remember who you are!" What exactly that implies may vary from family to family. Several obvious lessons may be drawn.

The most apparent suggestion is this: remember that you are a child of God—a god in embryo, a god in the making! You should act as your Heavenly Father has taught you to act. You should also *not* act in a way that might *in any way* put the promises of God to you in jeopardy. You have been offered exaltation. God has said that His intent is to give you everything He has: knowledge, power, beauty, glory, and an eternity in His presence. Forgetting those promises places us at risk of losing those promises. Remembering how much is

at stake increases the likelihood that the inheritance offered will ultimately be received.

A second common meaning of the phrase "remember who you are" is that we are each children of a particular earthly family—a family with beliefs, standards, commitments, and covenants. The encouragement to remember is a reminder to live those standards and be true to those beliefs. However, it is also a reminder that the things we choose to do or say never affect just one person. Because we are part of a family (an earthly family and a heavenly or Church family), when we choose good, it reflects upon our parents, grandparents, siblings, and spouse—even upon the Church to which we belong. And when we choose to do or speak evil, it likewise reflects upon others. No one can sin in isolation. Others will inevitably be affected by our choices. Thus, whether old or young, we must always remember who we are—or, as a dear friend of mine often says, "Remember *whose* you are!"

৵ Remember ৎ

Who Your Children Are

Early *in our* marriage, my wife and I were much like any other newly married couple—poor. Scraping together the money for a date was not easy, and trusting babysitters with our infant children was difficult. In those first few years of marriage, we seldom went out without children in tow.

When our first child was about ten months old, we planned a simple night out. We would be gone for only three or four hours at the most. The babysitter we hired was a girl from our ward whose parents were dear friends we trusted implicitly. What added to our comfort was that our sitter lived only a block from our house and her parents would be home while we were out (in the event of some unforeseen emergency).

My wife gave the teen sitter, who was not a novice, detailed instructions, and then we left for our date. Not long after we had departed, the evening's plans fell through. We would have to reschedule the date. Thus, approximately forty-five minutes after we had left, we arrived home unannounced.

When I opened the front door, I heard our baby daughter screaming. I hurriedly made my way to her room, and the babysitter was nowhere to be seen. I opened by daughter's door and could immediately tell she had been crying for quite some time. She was beet red, and her face was covered with tears and mucus. She was physically shaking, and I was both bewildered and angered by the scene. I picked our daughter up, comforted her, and then began to walk through the house looking for her sitter. I located the young woman to whom I had entrusted my baby. She was lying on my bed, eating a plateful of food and watching TV. She had shut the door of the room she was in and also the door to my daughter's room. The walls of our old home were rather thin, so I doubt she could have missed the screaming—though she clearly was hoping I would give her the benefit of the doubt.

More than two decades later, I have not forgotten that experience. I remember how upset I felt that someone I had entrusted with my child's well-being had betrayed that trust and neglected my helpless ten-month-old baby. I remember thinking, *How dare she?* The Lord's words rang loudly in my mind: "It were better for him that a millstone were hanged about his neck, and he cast into the sea, than that he should offend one of these little ones" (Luke 17:2). I thought to myself, *If I'm disturbed by this deliberate neglect, how much more offended must our Father in Heaven be?*

Tragically, much abuse exists in our world. Little children are harmed in myriad ways, and the Lord's notice to the abusers remains in effect: "We warn that individuals who ... abuse ... offspring, or who fail to fulfill family responsibilities will one day stand accountable before God."[14] Thankfully, most Latter-day Saints understand the evils associated with physical, emotional, or sexual abuse. However, some forget that spiritual neglect is a form of abuse. Failing to teach children the ways of the Lord and neglecting to walk with them down that path is a form of spiritual abuse, which the Lord does not take lightly. He has declared, "And again, inasmuch as parents have children in Zion, or in any of her stakes which are organized, that teach them not to understand the doctrine of repentance, faith in Christ the Son of the living God, and of baptism and the gift of the Holy Ghost by the laying on of the hands, when eight years old, the sin be upon the heads of the parents" (D&C 68:25). It is our divinely given responsibility to rear our children in the gospel and to engender in them faith in God and His restored gospel. Ultimately, all those born into or adopted into our families are the children of God. He has given us stewardship over them for a time, but they are His. Like the babysitter who ignored the needs of my daughter, if we ignore the needs of our Father in Heaven's children—those over whom He has given us stewardship— then we should expect to be held accountable. As parents, we

must remember that our children are first and foremost His children. They are each a child of God. As we remember that and remember our stewardship to them and accountability before Him, we will do better in preparing them spiritually for the challenges that surely will come.

∾ Remember ᙅ

Your Family

With the ever-increasing popularity of social media, emotional infidelity is on the rise. Cyber affairs are mounting, and more and more cases of marital infidelity are having their origins on the Internet. Looking up an old high school sweetheart. Taking a peek at pornography. For all of the good the Internet provides individuals and the Church, there are latent dangers that lurk in cyberspace. Thus, remembering becomes paramount.

The words of Jacob in the Book of Mormon testify to the importance of remembering one's family. He lamented, "Behold, ye have . . . broken the hearts of your tender wives, and lost the confidence of your children, because of your bad examples before them; and the sobbings of their hearts ascend up to God against you. And because of the strictness of the word of God, which cometh down against you, many

hearts died, pierced with deep wounds" (Jacob 2:35). As the saying goes, "curiosity killed the cat," and it has been the end of many families and relationships as well.

Qohelet, the author of the book of Ecclesiastes, warned his reader, "Whoso breaketh an hedge, a serpent shall bite him" (Ecclesiastes 10:8). By application, there is safety to be found in building a spiritual hedge around ourselves. To not have such a hedge around our weaknesses is to place us in danger of being bitten by the serpent—Lucifer, Beelzebub, the devil, the great destroyer of the souls of men. Marital infidelity often starts because we forget our family. Pictures and physical reminders of our spouses and children serve as a hedge that can keep the adversary out. Placing a photo of loved ones next to a computer monitor (or as the desktop background or screensaver) can do much to dissuade the use of pornography. Constant reminders of those we love can limit the likelihood that we will forget our covenants and the consequences that inevitably follow all serious sins.

✣ Remember ✤

The Counsel of Your Parents

lmost every one of us goes through a stage of immaturity wherein we think our parents are out of touch with reality, that they simply don't "get it." Ideally, every one of us also lives long enough to go through a stage of maturation wherein we realize, "Oh my heavens! My parents were right; I'm the one who was an idiot!"

It is imperative that young people remember Mom and Dad have already lived through the stage of life that their children are currently going through. In many cases, the parents have already made the mistakes their children are about to make. They have already been through the "school of hard knocks" and can provide some wise, sound, and tested advice on what works and what does not. When the Lord commanded, "Honour thy father and thy mother: that thy days may be long upon the land" (Exodus 20:12),

He wasn't suggesting that you should honor your parents so they'll let you live to see another day. Rather, He was informing us that by honoring and heeding the advice of our parents, we would successfully navigate many of the dangers of the mortal experience. Through prayerfully considering their counsel, we can avoid much of the heartache the world offers those who try to "go it alone."

In his December 1995 interview with President Gordon B. Hinckley, Mike Wallace from *60 Minutes* conveyed what he considered to be the opinion of some that the Church shouldn't be run by old, out-of-touch men. He said, "There are those who say, 'This is a gerontocracy. This is a church run by old men.'" President Hinckley then quipped, "Isn't it wonderful to have a man of maturity at the head—a man of judgment who isn't blown about by every wind of doctrine?"[15] No matter how old we are, each of us would do well to remember that our parents aren't as "out of touch" or "dumb" as we once thought they were. The world of their youth was not the world of ours, but they have invaluable experience and the wisdom of years, which makes the prayerful consideration of their views the wisest path to take.

ᴖ Remember ᴗ

To Love

Love is the essence of who God is. If we do not love, we are not like the Father and the Son. John the Beloved wrote, "He that loveth not knoweth not God; for God is love" (1 John 4:8). Being a Christian is first and foremost about love—even more than it is about our doctrine.

The earliest Christians were known for their love of each other. Indeed, the pagans often suspected people of being Christian if they were overly kind, generous, or loving. Unfortunately, in the society we currently live in, we find so many things to justify feelings of anger, hurt, or offense. Christians, men and women who should be the epitome of love, now seem to blend in with the rest of the world. Mother Teresa told of how a minister of state from Sri Lanka said to her, "I love Christ, but I hate Christians." When she inquired how that could be the case, he explained, "Because

Christians do not give us Christ; they do not live their Christian lives to the full." Similarly, Gandhi is reported to have said, "If Christians were to live their Christian lives to the full, there would not be one Hindu left in India."[16] What was it about Christians that these two men saw lacking? It was not their lack of belief in doctrine. It was their lack of love in living their lives.

As Christians—particularly as Latter-day Saint Christians—we must remember to love, especially those who are not very lovable. We should pray for Christ to fill us with love (Moroni 7:48) and to point out to us those who need our love. We must remember that we have been created to love and be loved. The surest way to make converts, improve relationships, and please God is to love purely and deeply—to love as He loves.

∾ Remember ∽

To Forgive

Anciently, numbers were viewed as highly symbolic and pregnant with meaning. The most common of symbolic numbers in religious literature and ritual is the number seven. It symbolizes fullness, completion, entirety, or totality. As a rule, multiples of seven carry the same spiritual or symbolic significance. The word for seven in Hebrew is etymologically connected with the words *full, satisfied,* or *complete.*

The Gospel of Matthew records a curious exchange between the Lord and Peter. The Apostle asked, "Lord, how oft shall my brother sin against me, and I forgive him? till seven times?" Jesus, drawing on symbolic meanings with which Peter would have been familiar, responded, "I say not unto thee, Until seven times: but, Until seventy times seven" (Matthew 18:21–22). Of course, Jesus was not saying,

"Forgive someone 490 times, and then you are released from any obligation of being Christlike." Rather, His point was that we must forgive all men completely, fully, totally, every time we have reason to be offended. Curiously, there is no caveat here that we need only forgive those who are repentant or those who acknowledge their trespass against us. He requires us to forgive all and to do so every time we feel that we have reason to take offense.

Why is the Lord so emphatic on this point? Because He knows that not forgiving someone has a cankering effect upon the soul. Each of us has likely held a grudge against another, or known someone who has, and thus has seen the damage such an action and attitude can have. When an offender causes hurt and you or I choose to hold onto that, the offender wins! He continues to have power over our lives and emotions. When we "cast" our burdens "upon the Lord" (Psalm 55:22), however, our hearts can be softened, our wounds can be healed, and the offender loses power in our lives.

The Lord has declared, "I, the Lord, will forgive whom I will forgive, but of you it is required to forgive all men" (D&C 64:10). He has also reminded us, "If ye forgive men their trespasses, your Heavenly Father will also forgive you: but if ye forgive not men their trespasses, neither will your Father forgive your trespasses" (Matthew 6:14–15). Christ does not ask us to do something He would not do Himself. In the midst of His darkest hour, and at the exact moment He was treated as cruelly and unjustly as any human could be, He prayed: "Father, forgive them; for they know not what they do" (Luke 23:34). He did not simply preach forgiveness; He lived it. And He has left "us an example, that [we] should follow His steps" (1 Peter 2:21). Remembering to forgive, and trusting that Christ can give us the ability to do so, brings power and peace to our lives. Forgetting this truth gives the enemy of all righteousness (Acts 13:10) sway over our lives.

৵ɔ ℛemember ℭ৵

To See Other People's Point of View

I *knew a woman*—a good, faithful woman—who seemed capable of only seeing her side of things. She earnestly believed that if someone did not see things the way she did, they must not understand her point of view. Thus, always believing that her perspective was right, she would push and push until others would give in to her or would withdraw out of frustration. Somehow, she was incapable of seeing the value or validity in other people's points of view. As a consequence, all of her relationships were rocky.

Communication is not about being heard as much as it is about hearing and understanding others. Certainly, we need to be able to express ourselves and feel that our opinions are both understood and valued. None of us, however, are able to see every aspect of a given situation. We must, as President Hinckley counseled, learn to "see the big picture

and cease worrying about the little blemishes" that people manifest.[17] We must remember, just as in an automobile accident, various witnesses provide different perspectives. So also in life and relationships, the variation in perspectives brings richness, beauty, and protection—*if* we are willing to see the other side.

President Harold B. Lee used to say, "Survey large fields and cultivate small ones."[18] In other words, see the bigger picture and then go to work on your small part of that vision. As we interact with others—particularly those who see things differently than we do—we must constantly remind ourselves that we *do not* see every aspect of a situation. Others may know things we do not or have valid feelings we do not understand. Finding middle ground does *not* mean we are conceding. Rather, as we are open and receptive, it may only suggest we have chosen to hear and understand the views and perspectives of others—and this will always make for better decisions and richer relationships.

∾ Remember ᴄ∽

To Build Others

I once sat in council with a faithful priesthood holder who, in tears, told me of how, as a young man, he used his quick wit to emotionally destroy another boy. There was no malice in his heart, no spite toward the other boy. My friend simply liked to use his humor, and the other boy was a convenient target. Over time, the victim of the "humor" lost every ounce of his self-confidence. To this day, his abuser is filled with guilt and remorse for the irreparable damage done to one of our Heavenly Father's children.

The ability to see the humorous side of life is a gift—one that can help us endure those difficult times that come to each of us throughout our lives. Humor inappropriately used can, however, turn from being a salve for the soul to becoming a knife that pierces the heart. When we make others the object of our sarcasm or the butt of our jokes, or

make fun at the expense of another, we act contrary to our baptismal covenants. As Christians, we are to "mourn with those that mourn; yea, and comfort those that stand in need of comfort" (Mosiah 18:9). We must never cause discomfort or mourning.

The Savior edified all with whom He interacted—even the remorseful sinner. He corrected evil and inappropriate behavior when He saw it, but He had the ability to build up those whom He had reproved. As an example, in the famous episode of the woman taken in adultery (John 8), Jesus commanded her to "go and sin no more," but He also warmly told a woman whom He knew had sinned, "I do not condemn you" (John 8:11, Good News Bible Translation). The Savior was the epitome of "reproving betimes with sharpness, when moved upon by the Holy Ghost; and then showing forth afterwards an increase of love toward him whom thou hast reproved, lest he esteem thee to be his enemy" (D&C 121:43). He built others, knowing that by doing so, many would find the strength and motivation to change their lives for the better.

President Gordon B. Hinckley was known for his great wit and use of humor, which had the ability to endear him to us. And yet, I was struck with his tendency to use self-deprecating humor instead of humor that ran the risk of tearing down others. He looked for the good in others and sought to find a silver lining in every cloud. We must remember to build, not tear down. Amid all of the bad that we witness, there is so much good in the world and in the people around us. The Lord's love and President Hinckley's

manifest optimism are examples to us all of the power that comes from building others.

∽ Remember ∽

Don't Take Yourself or
Life Too Seriously

The *British poet* and playwright Joseph Addison noted, "Man is distinguished from all other creatures by the faculty of laughter."[19] And what a blessing that is. We live in great but complex times. As much as we should and do revere our great pioneer ancestors, the "trek" we have been called to endure is no easy task. Indeed, as Elder Neal A. Maxwell wisely observed, "All the easy things the Church has had to do have been done. From now on it is high adventure!"[20] So it is in each of our lives. And if we try to accomplish what the Lord has sent us here to do without the aid of a good sense of humor, we will most likely be overwhelmed by the task. I like how Sister Marjorie Pay Hinckley put it: "The only way to get through life is to laugh

your way through it. You either have to laugh or cry. I prefer to laugh. Crying gives me a headache."[21]

I suppose one reason so many of us struggle with feelings of discontent, stress, and unhappiness is our natural tendency to take life just a bit more seriously than we should. Our inability to laugh at ourselves and our circumstances can hinder our ability to have the joy God designed mortality to be (2 Nephi 2:25). The proverb reminds us, "A merry heart doeth good like a medicine" (Proverbs 17:22). In one of his last general conference addresses, Elder Joseph B. Wirthlin spoke of the importance of not taking yourself or life too seriously. He counseled each of us to substitute laughter for stress or anger. Doing so will have a healing and enlivening influence in and on our lives. Elder Wirthlin shared,

> I remember when one of our daughters went on a blind date. She was all dressed up and waiting for her date to arrive when the doorbell rang. In walked a man who seemed a little old, but she tried to be polite. She introduced him to me and my wife and the other children; then she put on her coat and went out the door. We watched as she got into the car, but the car didn't move. Eventually our daughter got out of the car and, red faced, ran back into the house. The man that she thought was her blind date had actually come to pick up another of our daughters who had agreed to be a babysitter for him and his wife.
>
> We all had a good laugh over that. In fact, we couldn't stop laughing. Later, when our daughter's real blind date showed up, I couldn't come out to meet him because I was still in the kitchen laughing. Now, I realize that our daughter could have felt humiliated and embarrassed. But

she laughed with us, and as a result, we still laugh about it today.[22]

Humor is a valuable antidote to the stress, frustration, disappointments, and embarrassments of mortality. When trials or disappointments come—and they *will* come—we each have a choice to make. We can either laugh or cry, feel frustrated or be filled with faith. But ultimately, the choice is ours—and the God-given power to decide is within each of us.

Not everyone can be the life of the party, but each of us *can* consciously choose to look for the humor in what we encounter. Elder Wirthlin suggested, "The next time you're tempted to groan, you might try to laugh instead. It will extend your life and make the lives of all those around you more enjoyable."[23] President Gordon B. Hinckley has suggested that we not simply learn to replace frustrations with joviality but actually become the type of people who see the world from a positive perspective. He counseled, "We need to have a little humor in our lives. We better take seriously that which should be taken seriously, but at the same time we can bring in a touch of humor now and again. If the time ever comes when we can't smile at ourselves, it will be a sad time"[24]

As we remember to seek out the humor and happiness in the day-to-day doldrums and difficulties, our Father will bless us to be healthier and happier, more energetic and more loved. And ultimately, we will be more functional tools in the hands of the Lord.

◈ Remember ◈

What You Felt for Your Spouse
When You Were Courting

L*ove is blind,*" as they say, and perhaps that's good! When a young man and young woman fall in love, so much of what concerns the world simply doesn't matter to them. Their hearts are twitterpated, and all is right in the world. Then reality sets in, and all of that sweet naïveté is dashed.

While most faithful Latter-day Saints enter marriage with eyes wide open, there may be some benefit to keeping them partially closed once you are married. Now, I am in no way suggesting we ignore bad or destructive behaviors in a relationship. What I am suggesting, however, is this: Life sobers us—perhaps a bit too much. Life is hard, as can be marriage, raising children, earning a living, and serving in Church callings. If we're not careful, we run the risk of

taking ourselves and life a bit too seriously and, in the process, forgetting the beauty of our spouses and those relationships that were once all that mattered to us.

The prophets have wisely counseled husbands and wives to continue the courtship once they are married. A weekly date is paramount, but so is serving your spouse. Daily doting can do much to keep a relationship healthy and happy. It requires sacrifice, but the payoffs are much greater than the payments! As President Hinckley pointed out, "Happiness in marriage is not so much a matter of romance as it is an anxious concern for the comfort and well-being of one's companion." He added, "If you will make your first concern the comfort, the well-being, and the happiness of your companion, sublimating any personal concern to that loftier goal, you will be happy, and your marriage will go on through eternity."[25]

Each of us would do well to remind ourselves of those things that initially attracted us to our spouses—perhaps by making a list of those attributes. In addition to the things that initially drew us, we should add the attributes that, over the years since our marriages, have developed, making them even more perfect than when we first met. Remember how you treated your spouse when you first dated—in an effort to secure him or her. That same conscious daily doting will do much to keep the flame burning—or to bring back that flame that once was so vibrant.

∾ Remember ∾

Everything God Does Is for Your Good

On *October 31,* 1838, the Prophet Joseph, his brother Hyrum, and several other men were betrayed by those who professed to be their friends. Though convicted of no crime, they were unjustly incarcerated in a dungeon jail in the town of Liberty, Missouri. There they remained for the better part of six months.

Shortly before their escape, aware that the Saints were suffering terribly, Joseph cried out in desperation, "O God, where art thou? And where is the pavilion that covereth thy hiding place? How long shall thy hand be stayed, and thine eye, yea thy pure eye, behold from the eternal heavens the wrongs of thy people and of thy servants, and thine ear be penetrated with their cries?" (D&C 121:1–2). Joseph was overwhelmed by the trials he and his fellow prisoners were being forced to endure. Equally disconcerting to him,

however, were the reports of what members of the Church were suffering while he was imprisoned and unable to help them. In response to his desperate pleas, the Lord tutored the Prophet with this counsel:

> If thou art called to pass through tribulation; if thou art in perils among false brethren; if thou art in perils among robbers; if thou art in perils by land or by sea;
>
> If thou art accused with all manner of false accusations; if thine enemies fall upon thee; if they tear thee from the society of thy father and mother and brethren and sisters; and if with a drawn sword thine enemies tear thee from the bosom of thy wife, and of thine offspring, and thine elder son, although but six years of age, shall cling to thy garments, and shall say, My father, my father, why can't you stay with us? O, my father, what are the men going to do with you? and if then he shall be thrust from thee by the sword, and thou be dragged to prison, and thine enemies prowl around thee like wolves for the blood of the lamb;
>
> And if thou shouldst be cast into the pit, or into the hands of murderers, and the sentence of death passed upon thee; if thou be cast into the deep; if the billowing surge conspire against thee; if fierce winds become thine enemy; if the heavens gather blackness, and all the elements combine to hedge up the way; and above all, if the very jaws of hell shall gape open the mouth wide after thee, know thou, my son, that all these things shall give thee experience, and shall be for thy good.
>
> The Son of Man hath descended below them all. Art thou greater than He? (D&C 122:5–8)

The Lord's instruction to Joseph was simple. In life we may be called to do difficult things. Indeed, it is a given that

each of us *will* be. However, Christ has endured more than any of us will *ever* be called to bear. Thus, while the Father has compassion on us during our times of affliction (Psalms 111:4), in the context of Christ's suffering, we really have no place to complain.

Equally important to Joseph, and to each of us, is the Lord's reminder that "all these things" that Joseph, the Saints, or you and I are called to endure "shall give [us] experience, and shall be for [our] good" (D&C 122:7). Or as the Lord elsewhere declared, "All things work together for good to them that love God" (Romans 8:28). Like the surgeon who cuts us with a scalpel in order to heal us, the Lord often requires that we endure difficult and even painful experiences so that we might be healed and strengthened spiritually. That which comes from God is good—no matter the nature of what He sends. As Father Lehi reminded his son Jacob, "All things have been done in the wisdom of Him who knoweth all things" (2 Nephi 2:24). Elder Neal A. Maxwell pointed out, "If we criticize God or are unduly miffed over sufferings and tribulation, we're really criticizing the Planner for implementing the very plan we once approved, premortally."[26] None of us wish to suffer, but we must be cautious to not reject the opportunities for growth and healing that are inherent in the experiences God sends us.

President John Taylor had what he called his "philosophy for trials." Innately optimistic, he described his philosophy in these words:

> So far as I am concerned, I say, let everything come as God has ordained it. I do not desire trials. I do not desire

affliction. I would pray to God to "lead me not in temptation, and deliver me from evil; for thine is the kingdom,
the power, and the glory." But if the earthquake bellows,
the lightnings flash, the thunders roll, and the powers of
darkness are let loose, and the spirit of evil is permitted to
rage, and an evil influence is brought to bear on the Saints,
and my life with theirs is put to the test, let it come, for
we are the Saints of the most High God, and all is well,
all is peace, all is right, and will be, both in time and in
eternity.[27]

If we are indeed "the Saints of the most High God,"
we must believe that "all is well" and "all is right" because
God is ever on the side of those who strive to do His will.
In the context of trials and life's frustrations, we would each
be blessed by remembering that all God calls us to endure
will ultimately be for our benefit and blessing. And in all our
struggles, let us remember His promise: "I will not leave you
comfortless: I will come to you" (John 14:18).

☙ Remember ❧

What Truly Matters in Life

A *passage from the* canon of Taoism offers some
profound counsel for those of us who live in developed countries: "It is easier to carry a cup that is
empty than it is to carry one that is full. . . . The more riches
you have, the harder it is to protect them" (*Tao Te Ching*, 9).

Westerners often forget that they are among the wealth-
iest people in the world. Indeed, even the poorest person
living in a western nation likely has more personal wealth
and possessions than some of the richest individuals in
third-world countries. Yet, we tend to never really be satisfied; we never seem to have enough. Ironically, children with
the messiest bedrooms are often from the most affluent of
homes. They are expected to be stewards over all that they
possess, and yet the more they possess, the harder it is for
them to be responsible for all of it. So it is with adults and

their personal wealth: the more we have, the harder it is to protect it—from others, from taxes, from mismanagement. Most of us would be better off if we poured out a little bit of what we carry in our "monetary cup." The vast majority of us have sufficient for our needs, and then some.

As the popular colloquialism goes, "The important things in life are not things." Money ultimately doesn't matter. Yes, we need to have food, clothing, shelter, and transportation. However, because of government agencies and religious organizations, most in this country need never go without the basic necessities of life. What is of real concern, however, is that so many of us who have plenty of the physical things of life forget that all that really matters are relationships: our relationships with God, with our spouses, with our children, and with those in our circles of family and friends. We must never forget that lives of holiness—lives that reach out to others, ministering to their needs—are all that matter. The clothes we wear, the cars we drive, the jobs we work—each of these are things we cannot take with us into the next life. In the worlds of Elder Neal A. Maxwell, some things simply will not make it through "celestial customs."[28] At the Judgment Day, the Lord will be primarily concerned with the degree to which you and I lived a loving, holy, and faithful life. The other things will simply not matter. This we must constantly remember!

Remember

∽ Church Service ∽

☙ *Remember* ❧

Not Everyone Is Where
You Are Spiritually

W**ard and stake** leaders often find it frustrating that those with whom they serve do not share their same urgency, vision, or love for the work. Similarly, many parents struggle with children who simply don't seem to get what all the hubbub is about when it comes to Church things. In both cases, the frustration and disappointment of the leader or parent can manifest itself as condescension and a holier-than-thou attitude, which then hinders the Spirit and distances those for whom we have stewardship. Satan may actually use our zeal for God's work and our love for the gospel as a tool to hinder the holiness we're seeking to establish.

It is imperative that leaders in wards, stakes, and families remember that those whom they lead are seldom in the same

place they are spiritually. I heard a priesthood "leader" once say, "I don't ask anything of them that I would not ask of myself." If Jesus applied that same standard to this "leader," the brother would be damned! As a parent or leader, it is inappropriate to expect of others what you expect of yourself. Most children aren't where their parents are spiritually, and most members aren't where their stake president is spiritually—which is why the Lord has placed them in the presiding or parenting positions He has.

The Prophet Joseph noted that if Jesus appears "to a little child, He will adapt Himself to the language and capacity of a little child."[29] Similarly, in the parable of the talents (Matthew 25:15–30), Jesus offers each the same reward—exaltation—but He does not give each the same stewardship or gifts. We must learn from Christ's example and only expect of children what children are capable of. Similarly, we must expect of those with different "talents" and stewardships only what they can bear. As leaders in our homes, wards, and stake, we must remember this, lest our zeal become a tool in the hand of the devil.

↜ Remember ↝
Your Duty

I n one of the greatest revelations on the priesthood given in this dispensation, the Lord warned, "Wherefore, now let every man learn his duty, and to act in the office in which he is appointed, in all diligence. He that is slothful shall not be counted worthy to stand, and he that learns not his duty and shows himself not approved shall not be counted worthy to stand. Even so. Amen" (D&C 107:99–100).

Duty is not solely an obligation of the priesthood. By virtue of covenants made at baptism, every Latter-day Saint has duties to the Lord and His children. In addition, when you or I accept a Church calling, we take upon ourselves duties associated with the calling. If I agree to serve as a Primary teacher, I have a duty to those children. If I accept a calling as an elders quorum or a Relief Society president, I have duties to those within my stewardship. If I receive

an assignment as a home or visiting teacher, I have duties and responsibilities associated with that assignment. If I am called to serve in the Sunday School presidency of my ward, there are associated duties that become mine by virtue of my having accepted that assignment. To accept a calling or assignment and then not carry it out to the best of our ability constitutes a sin. In so doing, we let the Lord down, but we also rob His children (for whom we had stewardship) of blessings the Lord had designed should come to them through us. President Thomas S. Monson taught, "Duty is not merely doing the thing we ought to do, but doing it when we should, whether we like it or not. . . . I believe we should have an attitude of willingness—even anxiousness—to learn our duty, to do our duty, and to put a touch of quality on the work we produce."[30]

In the vision of the three degrees of glory, the Lord spoke of those in the terrestrial kingdom as being "they who are not valiant" and thus "obtain not the crown over the kingdom of our God" (D&C 76:79). The degree to which a ward or stake successfully functions, and the degree to which its members are blessed, is determined largely by the degree those who have been given duties fulfill them with valiance and the guidance of the Spirit. If we do not regularly remember those for whom the Lord has given us charge, how can we expect Him to remember us? As Latter-day Saints, we must be better at learning our duty, and then remembering to perform it. We can remember to set aside time *each week* to work on our duty and to contemplate those for whom we have stewardship. "Doing good is a pleasure, a joy beyond measure, a blessing of duty and love."[31]

ᔆ Remember ᔆ

To Testify

I n the December 1832 revelation known as the "olive leaf," the Lord informed the members of the Church, "Behold, I sent you out to testify and warn the people, and it becometh every man who hath been warned to warn his neighbor" (D&C 88:81). While this rather famous verse is traditionally directed toward missionaries, its application is much broader than that.

Missionaries are to testify and warn those they teach. But leaders and parents within the Church must also take seriously the commission that God has "sent [us] to testify." We may naïvely assume that if someone is coming to Church, they know and believe as we do. We may also suppose that since we as parents actively participate in Church and live the gospel in our personal lives, our children know it is true and know that we know that it is true. However, neither of these assumptions are safe ones.

Leaders must remember to testify with boldness of the things they know and of the things the Spirit has directed them to say and do. They must not assume their flock knows that they know. The sheep need to hear the various shepherds the Lord has placed over them testify—and frequently.

Parents can more actively look for teaching moments and find ways to express with conviction the miracles they have been privileged to experience. I have myself been surprised at some of the things I assumed my children knew about me, my testimony, and my experiences with the Spirit. To assume they know is to shirk one's responsibility, and it limits the opportunities for children to feel and recognize the Spirit in association with the words of their mother or father. When the stripling warriors stated, "We do not doubt our mothers knew it" (Alma 56:48), I suspect that knowledge came from more than how their mothers lived, but it came largely because of the power behind the testimonies their mothers bore.

While it may initially be difficult to find ways to testify in our daily interactions with our children or our flock, our effectiveness as a parent, leader, and disciple of Christ will be greatly enhanced if we remember this powerful principle.

∽ Remember ∾

The Name of Christ

The phrase "in the name of Jesus Christ" (or its cognate) appears more than 130 times in the scriptures. This is certainly one of the most sacred idioms we can utter, and it may be one of the most important.

In D&C 63:62, we are informed that "many there be who . . . use the name of the Lord, and use it in vain, having not authority." While we often associate taking the name of the Lord "in vain" with swearing, or using God's name as an expletive, this verse seems to suggest another way we may sin when we use the name of God. Here the Lord suggests that to invoke God's name in an authoritative way when one doesn't have His authorization constitutes a sin. Thus, the Lord warns, "Let all men beware how they take my name in their lips" (D&C 63:61).

By definition, when a Latter-day Saint says "in the name of Jesus Christ" at the end of a prayer or testimony, or as part of a priesthood ordinance, he or she is claiming that the words spoken are in accordance with the mind and will of God. Were Jesus here today, these words suggest, He would speak what I have spoken, testify of what I have testified, and promise what I have promised. Can there be a more sobering use of the spoken word? It is an audacious claim, unless the Holy Spirit has actually guided the speaker to so declare! Can we, with any degree of propriety, approach such a phrase with casualness in our voices or without conviction in our hearts?

Over the years, I have been saddened at the frequency with which I see members of the Church casually utter the name of Christ as they are in process of walking away from the pulpit—almost as though those words (at the conclusion of a testimony or prayer) mean nothing more than "the end." We must remember the holiness of that phrase and the sacred significance of uttering it and speak it only with conviction, reverence, and even awe. We are bold to speak in the name of the Lord. May we remember the significance of so doing.

✌ Remember ✌

To Counsel

In the book of Proverbs, we find this gem: "Where no counsel is, the people fall: but in the multitude of counsellors there is safety" (Proverbs 11:14).

It is not coincidental that we have presidencies in the Church. All presidencies typify the Godhead—and God counsels. He sets the pattern for us—in our Church callings and in our relationships. President Gordon B. Hinckley explained:

> No president in any organization in the Church is likely to go ahead without the assurance that his counselors feel good about the proposed program. A man or woman thinking alone, working alone, arriving at his or her own conclusions, can take action which might prove to be wrong. But when three kneel together in prayer, discuss every aspect of the problem which is before them, and under the impressions of the Spirit reach a united conclusion, then we may

have the assurance that the decision is in harmony with the will of the Lord. . . . Two counselors, working with a president, preserve a wonderful system of checks and balances. They become a safeguard that is seldom, if ever, in error and affords great strength of leadership.[32]

There is safety when Church leaders counsel with their counselors. And so it is with companionships and parents. Revelation and unity are as needed in a home and family as they are in a quorum or auxiliary. When a husband and wife, or a father and mother, have a significant decision to make for their marriage, home, or family, to act without counseling first would be to act precariously. The wisest decisions are made in counsel with others, and the Spirit of the Lord is more readily accessed through councils, whether on the family, quorum, ward, or stake level. We must remember, on things of significance, to counsel with those the Lord has given you as your counselors.

In addition to counseling with those around us, we would each be wise to heed the advice Alma gave to his son Helaman: "Counsel with the Lord in all thy doings, and He will direct thee for good; yea, . . . if ye do these things, ye shall be lifted up at the last day" (Alma 37:37). While the Lord has placed many around us as counselors and confidantes, our first and most sure source of direction and counsel must always be the Lord. In following His ever-available inspiration, we have the promise that we will be "lifted up at the last day."

❧ *Remember* ❧

To Follow Promptings without Delay

***E**ach of us* has heard miraculous stories of individuals who, heeding a prompting, saved a life, found a convert, or served as an answer to prayer. Indeed, I have myself had a number of experiences like this. Those who know the history of the Church quickly realize that President Thomas S. Monson is the typification of one who brings to pass miracles by heeding the promptings of the Spirit. President Wilford Woodruff and Elder Parley P. Pratt likewise frequently received promptings that, when followed, brought to pass great miracles.

Such promptings, so common in the life of President Monson, are a gift of the Spirit. However, they are not a gift reserved for the President of the Church or the General Authorities. Each of us, having the gift of the Holy Ghost conferred upon us, may receive such divinely sent direction

for those within our stewardship. For most, such promptings come and go—often unnoticed and therefore unheeded. If we consciously give heed to them, however, they will become stronger and more noticeable; indeed, they become a dominant means of communication between the Lord and ourselves.

The determining factor in these promptings developing from faint whispers of the Spirit to strong feelings of urging is our paying attention to thoughts and feelings that come and then acting immediately upon them. The Prophet Joseph taught, "A person may profit by noticing the first intimation of the spirit of revelation; for instance, when you feel pure intelligence flowing into you, it may give you sudden strokes of ideas, so that by noticing it, you may find it fulfilled the same day or soon." He added, "Those things that were presented unto your minds by the Spirit of God will come to pass; and thus by learning the Spirit of God and understanding it, you may grow into the principle of revelation, until you become perfect in Christ Jesus."[33]

The key is to remember from whence these feelings and thoughts come, and then to remember to act immediately upon them. This is the Lord's way of keeping us safe, and it is His means of giving us the power necessary to bless others.

❧ *Remember* ❧

It's Not about the Numbers

I *recently ran across* a program on the Internet that allows one to report home and visiting teaching without actually talking to a supervisor. While no doubt this was created to help expedite the work, I was a bit shocked at the thought that conversations about the salvation of those for whom we have stewardship could be reduced to clicking a bubble on the Internet. Surely the worth of a soul is more than an Internet:

- I did it
- I didn't do it
- I made contact with my family, but I did not share a message

When I stand before the judgment bar of God, oh, how I hope that He doesn't decide my salvation based on such meager information. And how I hope wards throughout the

95

Church are not determining the needs of their members based on a tool like this.

Over the years, I've heard individuals complain that the Church has become too institutionalized. I have often retorted, "With fifteen million members, a certain measure of institutionalization is necessary." Truth be told, the Church is only as institutionalized as its members make it. Programs exist in the Church to encourage our faithfulness and active participation. But home teaching is not about the numbers; becoming an Eagle Scout is not about the rank achieved; and presidency meeting is not solely about fulfilling an obligation. Each of these elements—these programs—is simply an outward sign of an inward commitment, or at least they should be. If the goal is simply checking off the box, the effort will have fewer lasting consequences. If, on the other hand, the goal is the betterment of the self or the saving of a soul, then we have grasped why the Lord has given us "programs" and asked us to count "numbers."

As we function in our callings, attend our meetings, perform acts of service, or engage in the programs of the Church, we would be benefitted by remembering the ultimate goal of all we're doing. The programs of the Church are but a means to an end, and that end is eternal life. As we remember that perennial truth, numbers become souls and programs become tools to save those souls.

Live a Godly Life

∾ Remember ∾

To Pray

Over the years, as I have counseled with individuals who are struggling with some aspect of their testimony, the discussion invariably leads me to ask this question: "Are you praying regularly?" The answer is *always* the same: "No, I've kind of let my prayers slip a bit." It seems puzzling that anyone would be surprised that a lack of prayer could lead to a lack of testimony—and yet they often are!

Beyond the fact that neglecting our prayers weakens our faith, there are additional reasons why you and I must consistently pray. Relationships are based on clear and constant communication. Our most intimate relationships—those between spouses, between parents and their children, or between Christians and their God—only last, develop, and become meaningful if the participants spend time together,

ALONZO L. GASKILL

communicating with one another. Our ability to hear God's voice, or feel His presence, is something we earnestly need to develop. As our prayer life develops into a healthy and meaningful one, the spiritual promptings and personal revelation prayer was designed to provide become a reality. If, on the other hand, we limit the amount of time we are engaged in prayer, or we largely pray in hollow repetitions, prayer will become a burden and its benefits will not be realized.

We certainly should be on our knees several times a day. Some of the most productive prayer times, however, are when we are physically engaged but our minds are otherwise available to chat with our Father. When we drive somewhere alone, for example, rather than turning on the radio, take advantage of the perfect opportunity for prayer that presents itself (with eyes open, of course!). As we walk through a store or across a campus, a great opportunity to commune with God is available. While such conversations should not supplant our daily personal, family, or companionship prayers, they are nevertheless a powerful supplement. One reason they afford us such power is because they are non-obligatory. They are not commanded prayers, as are our morning and evening prayers, or our prayers over food. Praying when we are not expected to—when we have a few extra moments throughout our day—shows God we want to commune with Him, that is, be with Him, that we want to know Him better and feel His Spirit more deeply.

Prayer preserves our testimony, as we have already shown. But it also protects us in other ways too. It limits Satan's ability to tempt us (3 Nephi 18:18), and it gives us

the discernment necessary to "escape the hands of the servants of Satan" (D&C 10:5). In addition, as we sincerely and consistently pray before we act, the Lord promises to bless our work and actions to our good (2 Nephi 32:9), because in so doing, we will have His direction and inspiration in our work.

As corny as the old "prayer rock" was, the Lord instituted something similar in ancient times because He was concerned that His covenant people were forgetting to pray to Him and forgetting to ponder His words (see Deuteronomy 6:9; 11:20). Thus today, pious Jews throughout the world have a mezuzah (or prayer scroll) on their doorposts. Each time they leave or return to their place of residence, they are reminded (when they see their mezuzah) of the Lord and His blessings and of their need to pray. While I am not suggesting that Latter-day Saints should use a Mormon mezuzah, I *am* suggesting that we each need to create some personal means of reminding ourselves to pray and thereby to pray regularly.

Functional prayers do not happen when we are tired. If our prayers are said when the alarm clock jolts us out of our sleep or just before we collapse into our beds after a long day, we will not find prayer a source of strength or inspiration. We should say our morning prayers once we are fully awake (perhaps after our morning shower), and our evening prayers before we become drowsy (perhaps shortly after dinner). Doing so will enable us to be more receptive to the revelation prayer can bring, and will demonstrate to the Lord that we are doing more than simply going through the motions.

Remembering to pray, and seeking for additional opportunities to communicate with our Father, will enable us to sense more fully His presence in our lives. It will equip us to "conquer Satan" (D&C 10:5) and thereby preserve us from temptation and the potential loss of our testimonies. Who dares proceed in life without that protection?

∽❍ Remember ❍∾

Gratitude in Prayer

L ife is filled with twists and turns, and it is a dishonest man who claims that his life has in all respects worked out as he expected. Though those with a gospel perspective know that there will be trials, few of us can anticipate in advance the types of things we will be called to endure. Perhaps it is no wonder that in our daily prayers many of us are found on our knees pleading with the Lord for intervention, for some measure of healing of a heavenly kind.

The Lord reminded those who have faith in Him that "your Father knoweth what things ye have need of, before ye ask Him" (Matthew 6:8). Consequently, asking for His intervention seems less important than acknowledging His blessings so freely given. In section 59 of the Doctrine and Covenants, we learn that "in nothing doth man offend God,

or against none is His wrath kindled, save those who confess not His hand in all things" (D&C 59:21). Remembering our blessings and expressing gratitude for them—particularly amid our trials—is one of the most important practices of a true disciple of Christ. President Ezra Taft Benson was somewhat famous for his prayers, which were almost exclusively prayers of gratitude. Of this, President Gordon B. Hinckley stated, "As you know, I served as a counselor to President Ezra Taft Benson, and I was with him many times when he prayed. He did not ask for very much in his prayers. His prayers were expressions of gratitude. . . . Be grateful. Be thankful to the Almighty for His wonderful blessings upon you."[34]

When we remember to focus our prayers largely on gratitude, the Lord empowers us. He lifts our souls, even in the dark hours that inevitably come to us all. He enables us to see the bright side of almost any situation or circumstance. He equips us with the demeanor necessary to reach out and bless others. And He sanctifies us so that we begin to acquire His attributes.

✧ Remember ✧

The Captivity of Your Fathers

In a spirit of warning and prophetic counsel, Alma commanded his people to retain in their remembrance the captivity of their fathers (Alma 5:6; 36:29). Why focus on the "bondage and captivity" of those of the past? To some, the reason will seem obvious. More often than not, however, we fail to see the profundity in Alma's advice and thus we neglect to heed his counsel.

When I was four or five years old, I witnessed the arrest of my fourteen-year-old uncle. Though only a boy himself, this shirtless and shoeless youth was handcuffed and aggressively escorted to the squad car while I looked upon the scene, confused and afraid. Nearly a half-century later, I "retain in my remembrance" a vivid mental image of the event: where I was standing at the moment of his arrest, what he was wearing, and how those around me responded to this shocking

incident in our family. I was too young to fully grasp all that was happening, nevertheless, the experience left me a changed boy. My uncle's vice for which he had been arrested was substance abuse. He was using and selling drugs. I was not a Latter-day Saint at that time. The faith with which I was associated taught nothing akin to the Word of Wisdom. However, from that day and throughout the years leading up to my conversion to Mormonism, I was never tempted to use drugs, smoke, or drink alcohol. Owing that I was reared in a family of "smokers" and my parents owned a liquor store, I attribute my abstinence to one thing: I could not forget my uncle's arrest. Over the years, as I watched the "bondage and captivity" that came into his life because of drugs and alcohol, any temptation to partake was completely squelched by the reality that his "captivity" could become mine.

Remembering the captivity of our fathers offers us protection from their failings and sins. It is a vivid and practical way to see the consequences of sin without partaking of that which God has forbidden. As we remember the "bondage" those of the past have encountered through straying from God's path, we are given rather practical reasons for living more holy lives.

Appropriately, Alma also reminds us of God's mercy, long-suffering, and power to deliver our souls from the hell created by our sins and disobedience (Alma 5:6; 36:29). Thus, while his message is one of warning, it is also one of hope. Each of us sins. Each of us needs redemption. And God has provided the means whereby we can overcome not

only our sins but, in many cases, even our addictions. Christ is "the way, the truth, and the life" (John 14:6).

For the sake of our happiness and well-being, the Lord has warned, "Hearken, O ye people of my church, saith the Lord your God, and hear the word of the Lord concerning you—the Lord who shall suddenly come to His temple; the Lord who shall come down upon the world with a curse to judgment; yea, upon all the nations that *forget* God" (D&C 133:1–2; emphasis added). We often quote the colloquialism, "Those who forget the past are doomed to repeat it." It is a blessing to witness the mistakes of society—including the consequences of those mistakes—*if* we learn from them. If we forget God, however, we will bring upon ourselves the curses, captivity, and bondage of this lone and dreary world.

ᥫᏏ *Remember* ᏟᏅᎧ

The Importance of Personal
Scripture Study

O*n numerous occasions,* I have heard some member of the Church joke about how many times he or she has started the Book of Mormon without ever making it past 2 Nephi. Frankly, it's really not very funny! It is a sad indictment of the reader, a testament to the fact that too many of us read rather than study scripture.

In discussing difficult scriptural books, Elder McConkie emphasized our obligation to study, really delve into, the scriptures. In response to the question, "Does the Lord really expect me to understand the book of Revelation?" Elder McConkie wrote,

> Certainly. Why else did the Lord reveal it? The common notion that it deals with beasts and plagues and mysterious symbolisms that cannot be understood is just not true. . . .

> Most of the book . . . is clear and plain and should be understood by the Lord's people. . . . The Lord expects us to seek wisdom, to ponder His revealed truths, and to gain a knowledge of them by the power of His Spirit. Otherwise He would not have revealed them unto us. He has withheld the sealed portion of the Book of Mormon from us because it is beyond our present ability to comprehend. . . . But He has not withheld the Book of Revelation, because it is not beyond our capacity to comprehend.[35]

Regarding our need to understand the meaning of Isaiah's words, Elder McConkie conjectured,

> If our eternal salvation depends upon our ability to understand the writings of Isaiah as fully and truly as Nephi understood them—and who shall say such is not the case!—how shall we fare in that great day when with Nephi we shall stand before the pleasing bar of Him who said: 'great are the words of Isaiah'? . . . It just may be that my salvation (and yours also!) does in fact depend upon our ability to understand the writings of Isaiah as fully and truly as Nephi understood them.[36]

Elder McConkie's point is valid. Why would God give us scripture if He did not expect us to understand and apply it? That being the case, why are many of us scripturally illiterate? Largely because we read scripture, but not many of us study it. Perhaps we do so because we are simply so busy, or perhaps because we are only reading out of a sense of duty or obligation. Regardless, there is a real distinction between reading and studying scripture; the benefits that derive from the latter far outweigh those gained from the former.

How do we make our study of the scriptures more effective? Several things may make a difference. First of all, make the goal quality rather than quantity. In other words, rather than seeking to get through a chapter a day, plan to study for thirty minutes and simply read as much as you can during that time. If you find things you don't understand, focus on learning the meaning of those words—even if that means you only read three verses one day. Second, don't assume you have to discover the meaning on your own. Purchase a commentary or two and study where you can have access to resources like LDS.org. Third, as you study each day, do so with a purpose in mind. In other words, while in the scriptures, look for a verse or message in the verses you read on which you could turn around and give a spiritual thought, were you called upon to do so immediately after your scripture study that day. If you're attentive while you're studying, the Lord will bless you with insights and applications. Fourth, tackle the hard books. Make it a goal to read and grasp the meaning of books like Isaiah, Revelation, or Ezekiel. They'll take more time to comprehend. But in paying the price, the Lord will bless you with inspired insight and He will make scripture study enjoyable. Finally, since we have so much technology available to us in the modern era, consider writing your own verse-by-verse commentary on whatever book you're studying. This doesn't need to be a scholarly work. Just read and record what strikes you. If a verse brings to mind a quote or general conference talk, make a note of it in your commentary. If it reminds you of an experience you've had, add that too. What a gift to

posterity to be able to say, "Here's my commentary on the Book of Mormon that I have written over the last twenty years as I have studied that holy book." What better testimony could we give to our posterity than this?

As we remember to study and contemplate the Lord's words each day, we have the promise that His Spirit will fill our lives and temptations will be less enticing. Our trials will be less overwhelming, and our ability to find answers to our questions and direction in our challenges will be increased. As we study and contemplate, the love and strength of the Lord will be more evident in our lives. These are all things Satan does not want for us, but they are all things daily scripture study can bring.

☙ Remember ☙

Death

I*n the book* of Ecclesiasticus in the Apocrypha, Yeshua ben Eleazar counsels, "Whatever you do, remember that some day you must die. As long as you keep this in mind, you will never sin" (Ecclesiasticus 7:36). While a morbid fixation on death is never healthy, Yeshua's counsel here is actually quite valuable. We often commit sin because we believe we have time to repent. "I'll change later," we reason. But truth be told, none of us knows when our day of reckoning will come.

Recently, a twenty-seven-year-old friend of mine—a father of three young children—was killed in a tragic automobile accident. His passing could not have been more unexpected. Each of us no doubt has a similar story of the sudden, unexpected death of an acquaintance or loved one. Forgetting that each of us will die—and many unexpectedly—is

a dangerous way to live life. Alma's counsel is wise advice to all: "Cast off your sins, and [do] not procrastinate the day of your repentance" (Alma 13:27). Other than the terminally ill, none of us has the ability to guesstimate with any degree of certainty the hour in which we will depart this life, nor how long we have before we will stand before our Maker to give an accounting of our lives.

We must not fixate on death, but we should daily evaluate where we are spiritually and remember that "if we do not improve our time while in this life, then cometh the night of darkness wherein there can be no labor performed" (Alma 34:33). If today were the last day you or I drew a breath, would we be sufficiently prepared to stand before our God? If the answer is in any way in question, we should sincerely begin to make significant changes before it is "everlastingly too late" (Helaman 13:38). Death is part of the great plan of happiness (Alma 42:8), as is that vagueness about when we will depart this life. Thus today is the day to remember our pending death and to prepare for our eternal life.

∽ *Remember* ∾

The Importance of Honesty

In *2 Nephi* 9:34 Jacob warns, "Wo unto the liar, for he shall be thrust down to hell." Though this passage is often quoted, its message may too often land on deaf ears. In my experience, the most common response to the temple recommend question "Are you honest in your dealings with your fellow men?" is "I try." What does that mean? How does one "try" to be honest? And what exactly keeps one from succeeding?

This almost cavalier attitude toward dishonesty was highlighted by Nephi, as he prophetically spoke of the last days:

> And there shall also be many which shall say: Eat, drink, and be merry; nevertheless, fear God—He will justify in committing a little sin; yea, *lie a little, take the advantage of one because of his words, dig a pit for thy neighbor; there is no*

harm in this; and do all these things, for tomorrow we die; and if it so be that we are guilty, God will beat us with a few stripes, and at last we shall be saved in the kingdom of God. (2 Nephi 28:8; emphasis added)

Nephi was shown by the Lord those who would live in our day and time. It was made known to him that many who lived in the dispensation of the fulness of times would reason within themselves that lying is not a major sin and that "God . . . will justify in committing a little sin" for "there is no harm in this." When a Latter-day Saint comes seeking a temple recommend and answers the question "Are you honest?" with the words "I try," it is difficult to construe that response as a yes answer. Rather than a "yea, yea" or "nay, nay" (Matthew 5:37), it feels more like a justification for "a little sin" (2 Nephi 28:8).

I suspect that those who answer "I try" are not grossly wicked individuals, nor pathological in their dishonesty. But I also suspect they are forgetting or downplaying the consequences of dishonesty—even in its most subtle and seemingly innocuous forms. The Prophet Joseph Smith is purported to have said, "No one can ever enter the celestial kingdom unless he is strictly honest."[37]

The Holy Ghost is the means by which we access the Atonement of our Lord. Through the Spirit, we are enabled to apply the blood of Christ. Through His blood, we are sanctified, making us both clean and also holy in our nature. The Spirit is a testator. It testifies of truth whenever and wherever it is spoken. When we are dishonest, the Spirit cannot testify of our words, nor convince those to whom

we speak of our holy intentions. Is it any wonder Doctrine and Covenants 42:14 instructs, "If ye receive not the Spirit ye shall not teach"? In addition to not having the force and power of the Spirit's testimony behind what we say, when we are dishonest in any measure, we also lose the sanctifying influence of the Holy Spirit. Consequently, we are not qualified to dwell with the Father and the Son.

I think it fair to say every faithful, believing Latter-day Saint wishes to be of use to the Lord in doing His work and building His kingdom. If we only "try" to be honest when it suits our needs, God's ability to use us will be greatly curtailed. However, if we remember to be "strictly honest" in all that we do and say, the Lord will endow our words and lives with a power otherwise unavailable.

❧ Remember ❧

Spiritual Experiences You've
Had in the Past

A s a convert to the Church, the day I *knew that
I knew* the Church is true is indelibly stamped in
my memory and upon my soul. For some, spiritual
experiences are commonplace. Wilford Woodruff seemed
to be such a man. He had *major* spiritual experiences frequently. However, most members of the Church believe not
because they have frequent, dramatic spiritual experiences,
but rather because they have had a series of subtle encounters with the Holy Ghost. These may come with some frequency, but individually, they may not seem that significant
to an outsider. Because the Spirit most often works in subtle
ways—as a "still small voice" (D&C 85:6)—it is quite possible to miss its manifestations. But it is also possible for the

spiritually alert to recognize its manifestations when they initially come and then forget those encounters over time.

Each of us will, at some stage in our life, experience challenges to our testimony. Those challenges may come because of some tragedy or loss. They may come because of sin. Some might have a crisis of faith because of some anti-Mormon claim on the Internet. Or perhaps a conversation with someone of a different religion might lead to some doubts. Regardless of the source of the doubts, we know the source of belief. God gives us reason to believe, and the availability of the Spirit to those who have been baptized and confirmed is such that frequent manifestations of the Spirit are available.

Nephi was chastised by the Lord for not recording the fulfillment of a prophecy of Samuel the Lamanite regarding a mass resurrection that would take place at the time of Christ's Resurrection. For those who knew of this prophecy and its miraculous fulfillment, it would ultimately prove to be a profound spiritual experience. However, Nephi and his associates had neglected to make a record of it (see 3 Nephi 23:6–13). The Prophet Joseph Smith was worried about offending the Lord because "he had given inspiration" to the Church "which they had not prized enough to record."[38] Like Nephi and Brother Joseph, you and I are given experiences—sacred, spiritual experiences—throughout our lives. Evidence that we hold them sacred and feel blessed that we have received them is found in our propensity to record them, no matter how subtle or seemingly insignificant they seem. Recording such experiences shows the Lord that we

recognize and are grateful for them. But making a record also accomplishes something else: in those hours of darkness or doubt, to which each of us is susceptible, having such a record serves as a reminder of how many witnesses we have had. A journal of sacred experiences serves to give us strength and encouragement in the face of doubt or adversity. And it leaves a record for our posterity—a testimony to them that we indeed knew the restored gospel was true.

Spiritual experiences have the power to strengthen us (and our posterity), but only if we remember them. The best way to remember them is to record them. Let us not forget the experiences of Nephi and Joseph, for one day we too will stand before the Lord, and He may very well say to us, "Bring forth the record which ye have kept" (3 Nephi 23:7).

⁊ *Remember* ᴄ

Lot's Wife

L ot, *a nephew* of Abraham, along with his wife and daughters, lived in Sodom. Because of the wickedness of that city, they were admonished by three angels to flee, as it was about to be destroyed (Genesis 19:1, footnote a; from Joseph Smith Translation). The angels gave them a warning as they fled, namely, head to the mountains, but *do not* look back or you will be consumed (Genesis 19:17). As God's destruction of the city began and Lot's family fled their home, his wife looked back upon Sodom and was turned into "a pillar of salt" (Genesis 19:26). Scripture records that Lot's wife was not the only one to look back at Sodom. Abraham also looked back, but he was not destroyed (Genesis 19:27–28). Looking wasn't the problem, however. Looking longingly was.

In scripture, mountains are standard symbols for the temple. Thus, fleeing to the "mountain" symbolically reminds us of our need to head to God's holy house so we might have protection from the world (so aptly represented by Sodom). "Looking back" symbolizes longing for something lost or something given up. Hence, Lot's wife's glance back was more than a simple look, but a longing for what once was. She left Sodom as a city, but Sodom was very much in her heart. Thus, though she headed toward the temple (or mountain), she had in no way come to love it as she loved the world (or Sodom). Elder Neal A. Maxwell explained:

> Many today are as indecisive about the evils emerging around us—are as reluctant to renounce fully a wrong way of life—as was Lot's wife. Perhaps in this respect, as well as in the indicators of corruption of which sexual immorality is but one indicator, our present parallels are most poignant and disturbing. It was Jesus Himself who said, "Remember Lot's wife." Indeed we should—and remember too all that the Savior implied with those three powerful words. While it was tragic for Lot's wife to look back, for our generation a hard look back at Sodom could save us from impending tragedies![39]

The more we love the world, the more we take upon ourselves its countenance—whether that be a darkness, a worldliness, lasciviousness, or some other trait. Similarly, if we love the Lord, it is His image we will begin to develop in our countenance (Alma 5:14, 19). In antiquity, pillars were often erected as memorials, reminders of some event or person. Lot's wife became a pillar (a testament or memorial) to her

sins, a reminder of what she loved and who she truly was. Such tends to be the case with all who give in to sin. Their lives become pillars, testaments, or memorials to the sins they have embraced and the consequences of such actions. Indeed, each life, once it is over, stands as a memorial to what that person really loved. So it was with Lot's wife, and so it will be for you and me. If we follow the Savior's admonition to "remember Lot's wife" (Luke 17:32), our souls will find salvation. If, on the other hand, we—like her—keep the commandments while longingly looking back at what the world has to offer, we to will stand as a memorial to blessings lost because of sins embraced.

৩ Remember ৎ

To Be Patient with Yourself

In *Shakespeare's Othello*, Iago says to his counterpart Roderigo, "How poor are they that have not patience! What wound did ever heal but by degrees?"[40] Of all people, one would think that Latter-day Saints would get this. Unfortunately, like anyone else, we forget that nothing worth having is had in a moment. One early Christian source noted the impatience of the first Christians in their pursuit of godhood. He wrote, "We cast blame upon Him, because we have not been made gods from the beginning, but at first merely men, then at length gods."[41] As you and I pursue that same lofty goal, too many of us lose patience with our imperfections, as though a gentle wave of the wand could turn the weakest of us into the greatest of us.

Elder Neal A. Maxwell cautioned,

Eternal things are always done in the process of time. Men are ripened in righteousness as the grain is ripened. Each process requires rich soil and the sunlight of heaven. Time is measured only to impatient men. *Direction is initially more important than speed.* Who would really want momentum anyway, if he were on a wrong course?[42]

We really must avoid a fixation with impatience. Satan uses this to discourage us, and impatience with our imperfections implies a lack of faith in the Atonement. ("Oh, great! Now I've discovered one more thing I'm delinquent in developing.") When we doubt that we're measuring up, more often than not we are fixating on how much *we* are doing rather than how much *Christ* is doing *for* and to *us*. Dare we criticize His progress with us? Would we be wise in saying He's somehow not moving at the right pace in perfecting us? The book of Ecclesiastes reminds us, "Better is the end of a thing than the beginning thereof: and the patient in spirit is better than the proud in spirit" (Ecclesiastes 7:8). We are wont in Mormonism to speak of "eternal progression." Let us not forget that we are each "in process." Our exaltation will be determined less by how far along the path we made it before we died and more on which direction we were facing. Remember, if our eyes are riveted upon the Lord, He will attend to our imperfections (Philippians 1:6). If our eyes are riveted on ourselves, however, we will find no end of deficiencies and no ability to correct them.

⁀ Remember ⁀

Christ's Example of Ministering

L eadership callings in the Church typically require that we have some administrative skills. Indeed, contingent upon the calling, an assignment in a ward or stake to serve in a leadership position may require a sizable amount of administration. The gospel, however, is ultimately *not* about administration; it is all about ministration.

To a group of scribes and Pharisees—"priesthood leaders" of their day—Jesus rhetorically asked, "What man of you, having an hundred sheep, if he lose one of them, doth not leave the ninety and nine in the wilderness, and go after that which is lost, until he find it?" (Luke 15:4). President Hinckley pointed out, "Conversion is never a mass process. It is an individual thing."[43] The Prophet Joseph taught, "Nothing is so much calculated to lead people to forsake sin as to take them by the hand, and watch over them with

tenderness."[44] Church leadership is about the rescue of and service toward the "one." If we allow our callings to become largely administrative, we've largely missed the point of Church service.

Regardless of our Church assignment, we must remember Christ's example of ministering. We can look for opportunities to reach out, to visit individuals in their homes, to seek out and bless or minister to the individual. Presidencies would be wise to schedule time every month, if not every week or two, to be out in the homes of those for whom they have stewardship. A leader who is in the home of one of his or her members is able to feel and discern things about that person or family that cannot be felt through a visit in the foyer at Church. And a family or individual who receives a visit in the home from a ward or stake leader—a visit made out of love and for no other reason—feels something about that leader's concern and care that could not be conveyed by a chat in the chapel.

We would do well to remember that, as leaders and as disciples of Christ, we are His face, hands, and voice to the members of our quorum, class, or congregation. Jesus's visible presence was less in the synagogue and more in the lives and homes of the saints and sinners—and so it should be with us.

~ Remember ~

That Your Temporal Gifts Do Not Belong to You

I*n what may* be one of the classic discourses in all of holy writ, King Benjamin informs us of our need to take that with which God has blessed us and be stewards over it, using it to bless His other children (Mosiah 4:16–22, 26). Benjamin commands us to administer of our substance to those who stand in need. Never, says he, "suffer that the beggar putteth up his petition to you in vain" (verse 16). Some will argue, "It is his own fault that he is poor. If he worked hard, as I do, he would have sufficient for his needs. So why should I give him what *I've* worked for when *he* makes little effort to pull his own weight?" (see verse 17). To this King Benjamin responds, "O man, whosoever doeth" or thinketh "this the same hath great cause to repent; and except he repenteth of that which he hath done he perisheth

forever, and hath no interest in the kingdom of God" (verse 18).

King Benjamin's reasoning is simple. None of us is self-sufficient. We all depend upon someone else for our existence, maintenance, or well-being. He explains, "If ye should serve Him who has created you from the beginning, and is preserving you from day to day, by lending you breath, that ye may live and move and do according to your own will, and even supporting you from one moment to another—I say, if ye should serve him with all your whole souls yet ye would be unprofitable servants" (Mosiah 2:21). We are "unprofitable" because each of us runs up a significant "tab" in sins—and we're incapable of paying anything on that tab. Thus, the Greatest of All came here, suffered, bled, and died so that the debt we have incurred could be paid and our damnation averted. In the words of King Benjamin, we're all "beggars" and are desperately dependent upon God "for all the substance which we have, for both food and raiment, and for gold, and for silver, and for all the riches which we have of every kind" (Mosiah 4:19). In addition to providing for us temporally, we constantly beg Him for a remission of sins, and, as undeserving as we are of that blessing, He gives it to us because we ask (verse 20). Thus, Benjamin says, since God gives *you* what you ask for (and yet don't deserve), you must not condemn others for asking you for things *they* don't deserve.

> If ye judge the man who putteth up his petition to you for your substance that he perish not, and condemn him, how much more just will be your condemnation for withholding

your substance, which doth not belong to you but to God, to whom also your life belongeth; and yet ye put up no petition, nor repent of the thing which thou hast done.

I say unto you, wo be unto that man, for his substance shall perish with him. (Verses 22–23)

According to King Benjamin, my temporal substance simply doesn't belong to me. *My* substance isn't actually *mine*. It belongs to God. He is the source of all. And in these verses, He is commanding you and me to freely use the temporal things with which He has endowed us to bless those whom He has placed around us, those who have needs (see also D&C 42:30; Galatians 2:10).

Some will say, "But I earned this. I worked hard for it. I amassed this through my talents, energies, and ingenuity." To this, King Benjamin would say, "No you didn't!" As noted above, God preserves our lives every day and gives us the ability to think, move, act, work, and speak (Mosiah 2:21). So, if we argue that we worked hard for something, King Benjamin would remind us that God was the one that *made it possible for us* to work hard. If He had not granted us that blessing—and to many He has not—then we too would be without the temporal things we enjoy. If God had not endowed you and me (as a gift) with the intellect He has, we would not have been able to develop it to our advantage. If God had not elected to have us born in a nation where an education is available and affordable, we would not have the opportunities that have been ours. So, even if we have worked hard, God is the one who has made it possible for us to do so—and has not made it possible for others to. Thus, to say "I have these talents because of *my* efforts" or "I have this wealth because of *my* hard work" is to forget that all of these things are really a gift from God. And just as He has freely given them to you and me, and endowed us with the ability to magnify them, He could just as easily take them away from us. To say these things are all *my* doing is to forget the following warning from the Lord: "In nothing doth man offend God, or against none is his wrath kindled, save those who confess not His hand in all things" (D&C 59:21).

As King Benjamin points out, though the Lord owes us nothing, He does desire to bless us, and especially as we give heed to this commandment. In Mosiah 4:26 we read,

> And now, for the sake of these things which I have spoken unto you—that is, for the sake of retaining a remission of your sins from day to day, that ye may walk guiltless before God—I would that ye should impart of your substance to the poor, every man according to that which he hath, such as feeding the hungry, clothing the naked, visiting the sick and administering to their relief, both spiritually and temporally, according to their wants.

As we begin to understand and retain in our remembrance the fact that *all* we have belongs to the Lord, He promises us sanctification and a remission of our sins. For even those small sacrifices we are called to make, the Lord blesses us. Truly God is *so* good and generous to us! How can we *not*, therefore, be good and generous to His other children?

✧ *Remember* ✧

The Pioneers

Latter-day *Saints have* a righteous obsession with the pioneers. As one who grew up outside of the Church, I was initially a bit puzzled by this. I do not have Mormon pioneer ancestry, and so I did not initially feel the connection and reverence that so many Latter-day Saints do for those who walked and pulled handcarts to the Salt Lake Valley. As I studied the history of those ancestors of our faith, however, I could not help but develop a love and devotion for them. I began to see them as icons of self-sacrifice and consecration.

Illustrative of why the pioneers need to be remembered by each Latter-day Saint is the oft-told story of the Martin Handcart Company. They reached the Sweetwater near Devil's Gate on November 3, 1856. The river was filled with chunks of floating ice. "Three eighteen-year-old boys

belonging to the relief party, came to the rescue; and to the astonishment of all who saw, carried nearly every member of that ill-fated handcart company across the snow-bound stream. The strain was so terrible, and the exposure so great, that in later years all [three of] the boys died from the effects of it. When President Brigham Young heard of this heroic act, he wept like a child, and . . . declared publically, 'That act alone will ensure C. Allen Huntington, George W. Grant, and David P. Kimball an everlasting salvation in the Celestial Kingdom of God, worlds without end.' "45

This is but one of hundreds of such stories. But the message is clear, and the pattern set forth. The pioneers are a symbol of sacrifice. They are a call to each of us to follow in their footsteps—being willing to lay down our lives for the gospel of Jesus Christ and for future generations who will be benefited and blessed by our sacrifices today. They are an invitation to all to forget self and go to work. They are a testament that exaltation is to be found in living life for others, even at great cost to oneself.

Sacrifice is central to the purpose of the great plan of happiness. Remembering the offering of the famed Mormon pioneers can give you and me the resolve to make our lives a gift to God and His children; in so doing, we will receive the ultimate gift—eternal life.

∽ Remember ∾

How Blessed You Are

One of the great hymns of the Restoration advises, "Count your many blessings; name them one by one, and it will surprise you what the Lord has done."[46] The line is catchy and the tune perky, but the counsel is often ignored. Do you actually count your blessings? Consider, for example, your situation with regards to each of the following scenarios:

- Do you have access to clean water every day?
  - 884 million people in the world don't.

- Do you have access to a bathroom?
  - 40 percent of the world's population doesn't.

- Do you have access to electricity?
  - 1/4 of the world lives without it.

- Do you have a roof over your head?
  - ¤ 1/6 of the world's population does not have adequate shelter.

- Do you have to go to bed hungry each night?
  - ¤ 22,000 children a day die because they are undernourished.

- Do you have a means of financial support?
  - ¤ 80 percent of humanity lives on less than $10 a day.

- Do you have access to an education?
  - ¤ 72 million grade school-age children do not have access to an education.

- In an emergency, would you have access to health care?
  - ¤ Any American can walk into an emergency room and get basic health care.

- Are you allowed to worship God according to the dictates of your conscience?
  - ¤ More than 400 Christians a day are put to death for their faith.[47]

This is but a sampling of the many blessings each of us enjoy every day—blessings that we often take for granted. Ingratitude is a sin, and it causes the withdrawal of God's Spirit from our lives. If you are able to own and read a book, you are most likely among the most blessed humans to ever live upon the earth. In all probability, you have access to more of God's gifts and blessings than 95 percent of the world's population.

Each of us can take seriously the invitation to count our many blessings. We can remember how good God has been to us. And during those times of disappointment or distress, we can take stock of all we have, all with which we have been blessed. May we never forget that God has spared you and me from the vast majority of trials the rest of the world has had to face. As the Psalmist has declared, "His merciful kindness is great toward us. . . . Praise ye the Lord" (Psalm 117:2).

✺ *Remember* ✺

That Happiness Is a Choice

Without some *clarification,* this is a potentially offensive declaration. I am well aware that there are those who, for example, struggle with clinical depression and for whom happiness is *not* a matter of choice. For those individuals, we must love, pray, and offer our sincere support and compassion. To downplay their trials would constitute a sin. Clichés can be annoying and often appear to view genuine tragedies with a Pollyanna optimism that is at the very least insensitive, if not downright offensive. Having said that, there is truth to the famed claim, "We cannot cure the world of sorrows, but we can choose to live in joy." I have known individuals with terminal cancer who have an optimism that many in good health struggle to muster. I have known individuals who have suffered incomprehensible financial reversals who, like Job, happily declare,

"The Lord gave, and the Lord hath taken away; blessed be the name of the Lord" (Job 1:21). I have known individuals who have lost a child or spouse in a tragic accident and yet have—with optimism in their voice—declared their joy in knowing they will see their loved one again.

Everyone suffers, no matter how righteous they are or how filled with faith they are. Suffering is part of life, requisite for godly growth. We have no power to prevent it, nor would doing so bring helpful or healthy outcomes. Again, we are reminded of the truism, "Life isn't about waiting for the storm to pass; it's about learning to dance in the rain."[48] Faith amid opposition is certainly a gift of the Spirit. Each of us has the ability to plead with the Lord for that gift. We cannot control much of what life sends our way, but we can choose how we will respond to it.

We would each do well to remember that when we despair, we turn our backs on God. Yet, as we keep in the forefront of our minds the overarching plan of salvation, difficulties and trials can be seen in context, and we can remain happy no matter what our situation.

❧ *Notes* ❧

1. Spencer W. Kimball, "Circles of Exaltation," an address to religious educators, June 28, 1968, in *Charge to Religious Educators*, 2d. edition (Salt Lake City: The Church of Jesus Christ of Latter-day Saints, 1982), 12.

2. Spencer W. Kimball, *The Teachings of Spencer W. Kimball*, edited by Edward L. Kimball (Salt Lake City: Bookcraft, 1998), 112–13.

3. Henry B. Eyring, "Recognize, Remember, and Give Thanks," *Ensign*, August 2013, 4.

4. Harold B. Lee, *The Teachings of Harold B. Lee*, edited by Clyde J. Williams (Salt Lake City: Bookcraft, 1998), 82; emphasis added.

5. Joseph F. Smith, *Gospel Doctrine* (Salt Lake City: Bookcraft, 1998), 116–17.

6. First Presidency letter, March 19, 1970; emphasis added. See also *Church Handbook of Instructions: Book 1* (Salt Lake City: The Church of Jesus Christ of Latter-day Saints, 2010), s.v. 14.4.1, 125.

7. Joseph Smith, cited by John Taylor, in *Journal of Discourses*, 10:57–58.

8. Joseph Smith, *Teachings of the Prophet Joseph Smith*, compiled by Joseph Fielding Smith (Salt Lake City: Deseret Book, 1976), 367.

9. Augustine, "Sermons," in Joseph T. Lienhard, ed., *Ancient Christian Commentary on Scripture: Exodus, Leviticus, Numbers, Deuteronomy* (Downers Grove, IL: InterVarsity Press, 2001), 104.

10. "Follow the Prophet," *Children's Songbook*, 110; emphasis added.

11. Hugh Nibley, "Work We Must, but the Lunch Is Free," in *Approaching Zion* (Salt Lake City, UT: Deseret Book and the Foundation for Ancient Research and Mormon Studies, 1989), 202.

12. Blane M. Yorgason and Brenton G. Yorgason, *Becoming* (Salt Lake City, UT: Deseret Book, 1986), 156.

13. Bruce R. McConkie, *Doctrinal New Testament Commentary,* three volumes (Salt Lake City, UT: Bookcraft, 1987–88), 2:322.

14. "The Family: A Proclamation to the World," *Ensign*, November 1995, 102, para. 8.

15. "Excerpts from an Interview with Mike Wallace of 60 Minutes," December 18, 1995, cited in *Discourses of President Gordon B. Hinckley*, two volumes (Salt Lake City, UT: The Church of Jesus Christ of Latter-day Saints, 2004–05), 1:614.

16. See Mother Teresa, *Where There Is Love, There Is God*, Brian Kolodiejchuk, editor (New York: Image, 2010), 349.

17. Gordon B. Hinckley, *Teachings of Gordon B. Hinckley* (Salt Lake City, UT: Deseret Book, 1997), 430.

18. See *The Church News*, Conference Issues, April 8, 1995, 14.

19. Joseph Addison, *The Spectator*, September 26, 1712, no. 494.

20. Neal A. Maxwell, in Cory H. Maxwell, ed., *The Neal A. Maxwell Quote Book* (Salt Lake City, UT: Bookcraft, 1997), 48.

21. Quoted in Virginia H. Pearce, ed., *Glimpses into the Life and Heart of Marjorie Pay Hinckley* (Salt Lake City, UT: Deseret Book, 1999), 107.

22. Joseph B. Wirthlin, "Come What May and Love It," *Ensign*, November 2008, 26–27.

23. Wirthlin (2008), 27.

24. Gordon B. Hinckley, "Excerpts from Recent Address of President Gordon B. Hinckley," *Ensign*, October 1996, 73.

25. Gordon B. Hinckley, *Teachings of Gordon B. Hinckley* (Salt Lake City, UT: Deseret Book, 1997), 325, 329.

26. Neal A. Maxwell, *That Ye May Believe* (Salt Lake City, UT: Bookcraft, 1992), 10.

27. John Taylor, *The Gospel Kingdom* (Salt Lake City, UT: Bookcraft, 1998), 332–33.

28. See Neal A. Maxwell, "Why Not Now?" *Ensign*, November 1974, 12.

29. Joseph Smith, *Teachings of the Prophet Joseph Smith*, compiled by Joseph Fielding Smith (Salt Lake City, UT: Deseret Book, 1976), 162.

30. Thomas S. Monson, *Teachings of Thomas S. Monson*, compiled by Lynne F. Cannegieter (Salt Lake City, UT: Deseret Book, 2011), 93, 94.

31. "Have I Done Any Good?" *Hymns*, no. 223.

32. Gordon B. Hinckley, "'In . . . Counsellors There Is Safety,'" *Ensign*, November 1990, 50.

33. Joseph Smith, *Teachings of the Prophet Joseph Smith*, compiled by Joseph Fielding Smith (Salt Lake City, UT: Deseret Book, 1976), 151.

34. Gordon B. Hinckley, *Teachings of Gordon B. Hinckley* (Salt Lake City, UT: Deseret Book, 1997), 250.

35. Bruce R. McConkie, "Understanding the Book of Revelation," *Ensign*, September 1975, 87.

36. Bruce R. McConkie, "Keys to Understanding Isaiah," *Ensign*, October 1973, 78, 81.

37. See Truman G. Madsen, *Joseph Smith the Prophet* (Salt Lake City, UT: Bookcraft, 1989), 104.

38. See Truman G. Madsen, *Joseph Smith the Prophet* (Salt Lake City, UT: Bookcraft, 1989), 110–11.

39. Neal A. Maxwell, *Look Back at Sodom* (Salt Lake City, UT: Bookcraft, 1975), introduction.

40. William Shakespeare, *Othello*, act II, scene 3.

41. Irenaeus of Lyons (circa A.D. 135–202), "Against Heresies," book 4, chapter 38, verse 4, in Alexander Roberts and James Donaldson, *Ante-Nicene Fathers*, ten volumes (Peabody, MA: Hendrickson Publishers, 1994), 1:522.

42. Neal A. Maxwell, *Of One Heart—The Glory of the City of Enoch* (Salt Lake City, UT: Deseret Book, 1975), 35; emphasis added.

43. Gordon B. Hinckley, *Teachings of Gordon B. Hinckley* (Salt Lake City, UT: Deseret Book, 1998), 142.

44. Joseph Smith, *The Teachings of Joseph Smith*, edited by Larry E. Dahl and Donald Q. Cannon (Salt Lake City, UT: Bookcraft, 1998), 247.

45. LeRoy R. Hafen and Ann W. Hafen, *Handcarts to Zion: The Story of a Unique Western Migration, 1856–1860* (Glendale, CA: Arthur H. Clark Company, 1950), 132–33.

46. "Count Your Blessings," *Hymns*, no. 241.

47. All stats can be found at "Poverty Facts and Stats," *Global Issues*, last modified January 7, 2013, accessed February 17, 2015, http://www.globalissues.org/article/26/poverty-facts-and-stats.

48. Vivian Greene, viviangreene.com, accessed February 26, 2014, www.viviangreene.com.

⌒ *Bibliography* ⌒

Augustine. "Sermons." Edited by Joseph T. Lienhard. *Ancient Christian Commentary on Scripture: Exodus, Leviticus, Numbers, Deuteronomy.* Downers Grove, IL: InterVarsity Press, 2001.

Church Handbook of Instructions: Book 1. Salt Lake City, UT: The Church of Jesus Christ of Latter-day Saints, 2010.

Eyring, Henry B. "Recognize, Remember, and Give Thanks." *Ensign,* August 2013, 4–5.

Hafen, LeRoy R., and Ann W. Hafen. *Handcarts to Zion: The Story of a Unique Western Migration, 1856-1860.* Glendale, CA: Arthur H. Clark Company, 1950.

Hiatt, Duane E. "Follow the Prophet." *Children's Songbook.* Salt Lake City, UT: Deseret Book, 1991, 110.

Hinckley, Gordon B. "'In . . . Counsellors There Is Safety.'" *Ensign,* November 1990, 48–51.

———. "Excerpts from Recent Address of President Gordon B. Hinckley." *Ensign,* October 1996, 73.

———. *Teachings of Gordon B. Hinckley.* Salt Lake City, UT: Deseret Book, 1997.

———. "Excerpts from and Interview with Mike Wallace of 60 Minutes," December 18, 1995. *Discourses of President Gordon B. Hinckley.* 2 vols. Salt Lake City, UT: The Church of Jesus Christ of Latter-day Saints, 2004–05, 1:585–618.

Hinckley, Marjorie Pay. *Glimpses into the Life and Heart of Marjorie Pay Hinckley*. Edited by Virginia H. Pearce. Salt Lake City, UT: Deseret Book, 1999.

Irenaeus of Lyons. "Against Heresies," Book 4. Edited by Alexander Roberts and James Donaldson. *Ante-Nicene Fathers*. 10 vols. Peabody, MA: Hendrickson Publishers, 1994, 1:462–525.

Kimball, Spencer W. "Circles of Exaltation," an address to religious educators, June 28, 1968. *Charge to Religious Educators*. 2d edition. Salt Lake City, UT: The Church of Jesus Christ of Latter-day Saints, 1982, 9–12.

———. *The Teachings of Spencer W. Kimball*. Edited by Edward L. Kimball. Salt Lake City, UT: Bookcraft, 1998.

Lee, Harold B. In *The Church News*, Conference Issues. April 8, 1985, 14.

———. *The Teachings of Harold B. Lee*. Edited by Clyde J. Williams. Salt Lake City, UT: Bookcraft, 1998.

Lienhard, Joseph T., Editor. *Ancient Christian Commentary on Scripture: Exodus, Leviticus, Numbers, Deuteronomy*. Downers Grove, IL: InterVarsity Press, 2001.

Madsen, Truman G. *Joseph Smith the Prophet*. Salt Lake City, UT: Bookcraft, 1989.

Maxwell, Neal A. "Why Not Now?" *Ensign*, November 1974, 12–13.

———. *Look Back at Sodom*. Salt Lake City, UT: Bookcraft, 1975.

———. *Of One Heart—The Glory of the City of Enoch*. Salt Lake City, UT: Deseret Book, 1975.

———. *That Ye May Believe*. Salt Lake City, UT: Bookcraft, 1992.

———. *The Neal A. Maxwell Quote Book*. Edited by Cory H. Maxwell. Salt Lake City, UT: Bookcraft, 1997.

McConkie, Bruce R. "Keys to Understanding Isaiah." *Ensign*, October 1973, 78–83.

———. "Understanding the Book of Revelation." *Ensign*, September 1975, 85–89.

———. *Doctrinal New Testament Commentary*. 3 vols. Salt Lake City, UT: Bookcraft, 1987–88.

Monson, Thomas S. *Teachings of Thomas S. Monson*. Compiled by Lynne F. Cannegieter. Salt Lake City, UT: Deseret Book, 2011.

Mother Teresa. *Where There Is Love, There Is God*. Edited by Brian Kolodiejchuk. New York: Image, 2010.

Nibley, Hugh. "Work We Must, but the Lunch Is Free." *Approaching Zion*. Salt Lake City, UT: Deseret Book and the Foundation for Ancient Research and Mormon Studies, 1989, 202–51.

Roberts, Alexander, and James Donaldson, editors. *Ante-Nicene Fathers*. 10 vols. Peabody, MA: Hendrickson Publishers, 1994.

Shakespeare, William. *Othello*.

Smith, Joseph. *Journal of Discourses*. Liverpool, England: Latter-day Saint's Book Depot, 1865, 10:49–58.

———. *Teachings of the Prophet Joseph Smith*. Compiled by Joseph Fielding Smith. Salt Lake City, UT: Deseret Book, 1976.

———. *The Teachings of Joseph Smith*. Edited by Larry E. Dahl and Donald Q. Cannon. Salt Lake City, UT: Bookcraft, 1998.

Smith, Joseph F. *Gospel Doctrine*. Salt Lake City, UT: Bookcraft, 1998.

Taylor, John. *The Gospel Kingdom*. Salt Lake City, UT: Bookcraft, 1999.

"The Family—A Proclamation to the World." *Ensign*, November 1995, 102.

Wirthlin, Joseph B. "Come What May and Love It." *Ensign*, November, 2008, 26–28.

Yorgason, Blane M., and Brenton G. Yorgason. *Becoming*. Salt Lake City, UT: Deseret Book, 1986.

∼◌ About the Author ◌∼

A lonzo L. Gaskill is a professor of Church history and doctrine at Brigham Young University. He holds a bachelor's degree in philosophy, a master's in theology, and a PhD in biblical studies. Brother Gaskill has taught at BYU since 2003. Prior to coming to BYU, he served in a variety of assignments within the Church Educational System—most recently as the director of the LDS Institute of Religion at Stanford University (1995–2003).

0 26575 14658 5